The Dysfunctional Family

How to Set Boundaries and Heal Yourself

Juanita E. Kelly

Bent Not Broken Books

ISBN: 979-8-9988568-0-8

ISBN: (eBook) 979-8-9988568-1-5

For rights and permissions inquiries, contact: info@bentnotbrokenbooks.com

Cover Design by: Bailey Tune

Published by Bent Not Broken Books

Barnegat, New Jersey

www.Bent Not BrokenBooks.com

This is Book One of The Becoming Series by Juanita Kelly.

This book is intended for educational and informational purposes only and is not a substitute for professional therapy, medical advice, diagnosis, or treatment. Readers are encouraged to seek qualified mental health professionals for support as needed. The author disclaims all liability for any loss or risk, personal or otherwise, incurred as a consequence of the use and application of any content in this book.

Printed in the United States of America

First Edition, 2025

Dedication

To my daughter, Clarissa, my greatest love, my brightest light, and my reason for pushing forward even in the darkest times. You are my heart walking outside my body, and everything I do is a testament to the love and strength we share. This book is for you and for every person who, like me, has fought to break cycles and build something better.

Epigraph

You may not control all the events that happen to you, but you can decide not to be reduced by them. ~Maya Angelou

Preface

If you're holding this book in your hands, chances are, you're looking for something more. Maybe you feel trapped in family dynamics that drain you. Maybe you've tried to set boundaries before, only to be met with guilt, manipulation, or resistance. Maybe you're just tired, tired of feeling unseen, unheard, and unimportant in the relationships that are supposed to nurture you.

I want you to know something: *You may be bent, but you are not broken.*

Family dysfunction can leave deep wounds, but those wounds do not define you. You have the power to rewrite your story, to break the cycles that no longer serve you, and to create a life that is built on respect, love, and emotional safety.

This book isn't just about identifying what's wrong; it's about helping you find away forward. It's about healing, setting boundaries, and stepping into your own power.

I believe in you. I believe in your ability to change your life. And I hope that by the time you finish reading this book, you will believe in yourself, too.

Contents

INTRODUCTION

I'll never forget the day I realized my family wasn't like the ones I saw on TV. I was 7 years old ,sitting at the kitchen table, trying to explain why I felt hurt by something my uncle had said. Instead of comfort, I was met with silence, a silence that spoke volumes. That moment was the first time I questioned whether my feelings mattered. If you've ever felt invisible in your own family, this book is for you.

What if the people who were supposed to love you the most were the ones who hurt you the deepest? For many, family is meant to be a safe haven, a place where love, trust, and support flow freely. But for some of us, family feels like the opposite: a source of pain, confusion, and emotional scars. You've felt the weight of dysfunction pressing on your chest, the sting of harsh words that linger long after they're spoken, and the hollow ache of love that feels more like obligation. Perhaps you've spent years trying to fix things, trying to be "good enough," quiet enough, or accommodating enough to make the pain go away. Maybe you've even convinced yourself that this is just how families are, that you're the problem, or that you don't deserve better. But deep down, you know something isn't right. You know you deserve more.

This book is for anyone who has felt trapped in toxic family dynamics, struggled with self-doubt, or questioned their worth because of their upbringing. Family dysfunction can take many forms, such as emotional neglect, manipulation, abuse, or simply a lack of healthy boundaries. It might look like a parent who criticizes everything you do, a sibling who constantly undermines you, or a family culture that prioritizes appearances over authenticity. Whatever your experience, this book is here to help.

I've walked this difficult path myself, grappling with the same questions and emotions that might be weighing on you now. I've seen the damage caused by those closest to me, and it made me question everything I thought I knew about love, loyalty, and identity. For years, I believed my struggles were my fault, that if I could just be quieter or more accommodating, things would improve. But they didn't. It wasn't until I stepped back and faced the truth about my family dynamics that I realized the dysfunction wasn't mine to own; it was a legacy I'd been handed.

The Purpose of This Book

This book is both a guide and a companion for your journey. Together, we'll explore what family dysfunction really is, how it shapes your life, and, most importantly, how to break free from its grip. You'll learn how to recognize unhealthy patterns, set boundaries that protect your peace, and rebuild your sense of self-worth. This is not just about healing from the past; it's about reclaiming your future and building a life where you can truly thrive.

Through a combination of personal reflections, psychological insights, and practical tools, I'll guide you every step of the way. My goal is to show you that change is possible, no matter how deeply entrenched the dysfunction feels.

What to Expect

This book is divided into sections, each designed to help you navigate a specific aspect of family dysfunction and healing:

- We'll start by uncovering the roles and patterns that have shaped your family dynamics.

- Then, we'll explore how to set boundaries, rebuild self-esteem, and navigate relationships with difficult family members.

- Finally, you'll learn how to create a healthier legacy, one rooted in love, respect, and authenticity.

Each chapter includes practical exercises to guide your healing, with prompts that bring your learning to life. These tools are designed to meet you where you are, offering guidance and encouragement as you move forward.

My Journey

Healing from family dysfunction is one of the hardest things I've ever done. It required me to make decisions that felt impossible, to let go of relationships that were draining me, to confront truths I'd buried for years, and to put myself first for the first time in my life. But it was also one of the most liberating things I've ever done. It allowed me to reclaim my identity, rebuild myself-worth, and create relationships that truly nourish me.

I share this because I want you to know that you're not alone. The journey ahead may feel overwhelming, but every step you take is a step toward freedom. You are stronger than you think, and you have the power to create the life you deserve.

A Message of Hope

This book is an invitation to see yourself in a new light, not as a product of your family's dysfunction, but as someone capable of breaking cycles, setting boundaries, and building a life filled with love and authenticity. You don't have to carry the weight of the past forever. You have the power to heal, to break free, and to rebuild your life, with courage, self-compassion, and the right tools.

As you turn the page, take a moment to reflect on what brought you here. What pain are you carrying? What changes do you hope to make? This is your journey, and it starts now. You set the pace. You define the milestones. And you are never alone. Let's take this first step together.

CHAPTER 1

THE IMPACT OF FAMILY DYSFUNCTION ON YOUR LIFE

Family is meant to be a place of safety, trust, and unconditional love. But what happens when that cornerstone shatters, leaving us unsure of who we are and where we belong? Dysfunctional family dynamics ripple through every aspect of our lives, shaping how we see ourselves, how we interact with others, and how we navigate the world.

Have you ever wondered why the people who should love you most have hurt you the deepest? Why do the very people you depend on seem to bring you pain instead of comfort?

The impact of family dysfunction isn't always immediate or obvious. It's subtle, like a slow-moving tide, gradually eroding yourself-worth, confidence, and emotional well-being. At first, it's almost imperceptible; there is a wave of doubt here and a ripple of anxiety there. But over time, you begin to realize that your sense of security has been worn away, leaving you feeling lost and unsure.

You might not realize how deeply these patterns have affected you until you try to build a life of your own and find yourself carrying invisible baggage from the past. The anxiety, the sense of dread that builds in the pit of your stomach, the confusion of not knowing who to trust, these are the silent tolls of family dysfunction, felt deep within but often unseen by the world.

I know this weight because I have carried it for years. Growing up, I thought the anxiety, self-doubt, and struggles in my relationships were just part of who I was. But as I began to unpack my past, I realized how deeply family dysfunction had shaped my inner world. Recognizing these patterns was painful, but it was also the first step toward reclaiming my life.

Myth vs. Truth:
Challenging Misconceptions About Dysfunction

Before we dive into understanding family dysfunction, it's important to address some common myths that can cloud our perception and prevent us from seeing the truth. These myths often keep us stuck in denial or shame, making it harder to recognize and address dysfunction. Let's unpack them one by one.

Myth: "If I just try harder, things will get better."

Truth: Dysfunction isn't caused by a lack of effort or love. It's often rooted in deeper issues like unresolved trauma, generational patterns, or unhealthy coping mechanisms. No amount of effort on your part can "fix" someone else's behavior or change the entire family system. Healing begins with recognizing what's within your control and focusing on your own growth.

Myth: "Talking about dysfunction is disloyal or disrespectful."

Truth: Acknowledging dysfunction isn't about blaming or shaming your family; it's about understanding the patterns that have shaped your life. Silence often perpetuates harm, while open, honest conversations can pave the way for healing. You can love your family and still recognize that certain behaviors are unhealthy.

Myth: "I'm overreacting, it's not that big of a deal."

Truth: If you're feeling hurt, anxious, or drained by your family dynamics, your feelings are valid. Dysfunction often minimizes or dismisses your experiences, making you doubt yourself. Trust your instincts. If something feels off, it's worth exploring.

Why This Matters

Challenging these myths is the first step toward understanding dysfunction and its impact on your life. By replacing misconceptions with clarity, you can begin to see your family dynamics for what they are, not as a reflection of your worth, but as patterns that can be understood and changed.

Reflection Prompt

Take a moment to reflect: Which of these myths have you believed? How might letting go of these beliefs help you see your family dynamics more clearly?

Personal Reflection

I vividly remember the day I realized how deeply my family's dysfunction had shaped me. I was trying to set a boundary with a close friend, and their reaction triggered an overwhelming sense of guilt and fear; my stomach knotted, my chest tightened, and a flood of self-doubt washed over me. It hit me like a wave: this wasn't just about the boundary, it was about years of being taught that my needs didn't matter.

Another memory stands out from my childhood. During a heated family discussion, I timidly offered a suggestion, only to be dismissed with laughter and a wave of the hand. The sting of that moment stayed with me, the flush of embarrassment, the sinking feeling in my chest, and the painful realization that my voice didn't matter. That moment taught me to stay quiet, to suppress my thoughts and feelings, believing they were unworthy of attention.

As I grew older, I realized that the patterns I had learned at home were still with me. The anxiety around asserting myself, the guilt when I tried to express my needs, and the fear of rejection all traced back to those early family experiences. Over time, I came to understand that my emotional reactions were not just my own; they were shaped by years of being told that my feelings didn't matter.

But something shifted. I began to see that my voice mattered, that my needs were important, and that I could choose not to carry the weight of those old patterns. Slowly, I've begun to unlearn those lessons, to challenge the voices in my head that said I wasn't worthy, and to rebuild my sense of self-worth. It hasn't been easy, but every step has brought me closer to the person I am today.

Healing is like tending to a garden. At first, the soil is rough and overgrown, full of weeds and roots that run deep. But with patience, attention, and care, the garden starts to bloom. And just like that, your sense of self-worth will begin to blossom, little by little, until you feel rooted in your own strength.

And if I can do it, so can you. Your journey won't look the same as mine, but the process of healing and reclaiming your sense of self-worth is universal. You have the power to rewrite the narrative of your life, just as I did. You are not defined by your past. You are not stuck in the patterns that have held you back. The strength to change is already within you, waiting to be awakened. It starts with acknowledging the truth and taking that first step toward healing.

How Dysfunction Shapes Your Inner World

Family dysfunction doesn't just leave a scar; it etches itself deeply into our emotional and psychological blueprint, affecting how we see ourselves, how we interact with others, and how we navigate the world. Let's explore the areas it affects most deeply:

1. Self-Esteem

Growing up in a dysfunctional family often leaves you feeling like you're never enough. Whether through constant criticism, neglect, or unrealistic expectations, your worth becomes measured by others' approval rather than your own sense of self.

Example: Maybe you were told to "stop being so dramatic" when you expressed hurt, leading you to believe that your feelings were unworthy of validation. You might have carried that belief into adulthood, questioning your own emotional responses. This internalized sense of worthlessness makes it difficult to form healthy, confident relationships and can leave you feeling like you're always falling short of your potential.

Sarah's Story: Sarah, a woman who was a life coaching client of mine, had always been told by her mother that her emotional responses were too intense. As an adult, she found herself questioning her emotions and feeling ashamed of her needs in relationships. She constantly sought validation from others, yet never felt truly worthy.

Reflect on this: Did your family's words or actions make you question your worth? What messages about yourself did you internalize? When you reflect on your life choices, are they truly yours, or have they been shaped by the expectations of others? How do you feel about the dreams you've set aside?

2. Emotional Regulation

Dysfunctional families often teach unhealthy ways to handle emotions, either by suppressing them or expressing them in destructive ways. This leads to struggles with anxiety, anger, or detachment in adulthood.

Example: If conflict in your family was always met with shouting, you may find yourself avoiding confrontation at all costs or mimicking those same patterns. Alternatively, you may avoid emotions entirely, leading to emotional detachment or an inability to express your true feelings, which in turn causes frustration in relationships.

When we grow up in environments where emotions were not openly expressed or were met with punishment, we struggle to recognize and express our own feelings. This leads to difficulties in relationships, as you might not know how to process or share your emotions in healthy ways, leaving you feeling misunderstood.

Reflect on this: How do you handle conflict now? Do you shut down, a void it, or react with intense emotion? How does this affect your relationships?

3. Identity and Autonomy

In a dysfunctional family, individuality is often stifled by rigid roles or expectations. This leaves little room for self-discovery or personal growth. The roles we are forced into, whether as the peacemaker, the scapegoat, or the overachiever, often define us, even long into adulthood.

Example: A parent who pressures their child to follow a specific career path might unintentionally teach them to prioritize others' desires over their own. These rigid expectations leave little room for you to discover who you truly are and what you genuinely want from life.

These patterns can stunt emotional growth, leaving you in a constant state of self-doubt, unsure of your true desires, goals, and even your identity. You may find it difficult to make decisions without fearing judgment or rejection from others.

Ask yourself: What dreams or aspirations have you set aside to meet others' expectations? When was the last time you made a choice based solely on your own desires and not because of outside pressures?

Psychological Insights

1. Attachment Theory

Attachment theory suggests that the way we form emotional bonds in childhood shapes how we interact with others in adulthood. There are four primary attachment styles:

- **Secure:** Comfortable with intimacy and independence.

- **Anxious:** Craves closeness but fears abandonment.

- **Avoidant:** Values independence and avoids closeness.

- **Disorganized:** A mix of anxious and avoidant behaviors, often stemming from trauma.

If you grew up in an emotionally distant or inconsistent family environment, you may struggle with trust or have difficulty forming secure relationships.

Impact on You: You may find it hard to trust people or push them away, fearing they will abandon you as your family did. These attachment patterns don't just disappear as you get older; they persist in your relationships unless you actively address them.

2. Family Systems Theory

According to the Family Systems Theory, every family member plays a role in maintaining the family dynamics. Dysfunctional families often operate in unhealthy patterns, such as:

- **Enmeshment:** Too much closeness leads to blurred boundaries.

- **Disengagement:** Too much distance, resulting in emotional detachment.

These dynamics can create emotional imbalances that affect your well-being.

Impact on You: If you were raised in a family where boundaries were blurred or rigidly enforced, you may struggle with your own sense of autonomy. You might find it difficult to differentiate your needs from others' or feel overwhelmed by others' expectations.

Practical Exercises

1. Family Dynamics Map

Create a visual map of your family's dynamics. Write down:

- The roles each family member played (e.g., peacemaker, scapegoat, caretaker).

- The unspoken rules that governed interactions (e.g., "Don't show weakness," "Silence equals agreement").

Reflection: How have these dynamics shaped your beliefs and behaviors? Are there roles you're still unconsciously playing today? What patterns would you like to change moving forward?

2. Journaling Prompts

- "What messages about myself did I internalize from my family?"

- "How have my family's dynamics influenced my current relationships?"

- "What unspoken family rules did I follow without question?"

- "What would my life have looked like if I had felt fully accepted and supported by my family?"

3. Affirmation Practice

Identify a harmful belief you've carried from your family and replace it with a positive affirmation.

Example: Replace "I'm not good enough" with "I am worthy of love and respect just as I am."

Practice repeating these affirmations daily to rewire your thinking and reinforce yourself-worth.

Hope for Change

The impact of family dysfunction is real, but it doesn't have to define your future. By recognizing the ways it has shaped your life, you gain the power to unlearn harmful patterns and build a life that aligns with your values and aspirations. Transformation begins with the recognition of where we've been. It's not about erasing our past; it's about taking back control, learning from those experiences, and using them as a stepping stone to create a life of purpose and joy.

The path ahead may not always be smooth; healing takes time, and there will be setbacks. But with each step, you are moving closer to a healthier, more empowered version of yourself. Remember, it's okay to take things one day at a time. The changes you are making today are the foundation for a brighter tomorrow.

What's Next?

In the coming chapters, we'll dive deeper into the patterns of family dysfunction, explore strategies for healing, and provide tools to help you rebuild your sense of self. You'll learn how to set boundaries, cultivate self-compassion, and create relationships that nurture rather than deplete you. Together, we'll uncover the strength within you to rewrite your story and embrace a life of authenticity and joy.

CHAPTER 2

WHY SETTING BOUNDARIES IS CRUCIAL

Imagine this: You're sitting at your desk, buried under a mountain of emails, client requests, and deadlines. Your phone buzzes, it's another message from a client asking for a last-minute change to a project. You want to say no, but the word sticks in your throat. Instead, you sigh and type, "Sure, I'll make it work." Later, as you sit at your desk, exhausted and resentful, you wonder why you couldn't just say what you really meant.

This is what life without boundaries feels like: a constant cycle of over-commitment, resentment, and burnout. Boundaries are the invisible lines we draw to protect our time, energy, and well-being. They're not about building walls but about creating space for what truly matters. And yet, for so many of us, setting boundaries feels impossible. Why is that? And how can we start to change it?

Myth vs. Truth: Challenging Misconceptions About Boundaries

Before we dive into the importance of boundaries, let's address some common myths that keep us from setting them:

Myth: "If I set boundaries, people will leave me."

Truth: Healthy relationships thrive on mutual respect. If someone can't respect your boundaries, they may not be worth keeping in your life.

Myth: "Boundaries are only for people who have been hurt or abused."

Truth: Boundaries are for everyone. They're a proactive way to maintain balance and prevent resentment in any relationship.

Myth: "I don't need boundaries, I can handle anything."

Truth: Everyone has limits. Ignoring them leads to burnout, resentment, and even physical and emotional exhaustion.

By challenging these myths, we can begin to see boundaries not as a source of guilt or fear but as a tool for empowerment and connection.

Personal Reflection

I used to think that saying "yes" to everything was the key to success. As a business owner, I wore my busyness like a badge of honor. I was the first one in the office and the last one to leave. I took every call, answered every email, and said yes to every client request, even when it meant working late into the night or sacrificing my weekends. I told myself it was necessary, that this was what it took to build a thriving business. But deep down, I was exhausted, resentful, and constantly on edge.

I remember one particularly chaotic week when I agreed to take on a last-minute project for a client, even though my team was already stretched thin. I spent days juggling meetings, deadlines, and endless to-do lists, all while trying to keep up with the day-to-day operations of my business. By the end of the week, I was physically and emotionally drained. I sat at my desk, staring at a mountain of unfinished tasks, and felt like I was drowning. I had given so much to my business, but I had nothing left for myself.

It wasn't until I started working with a business coach that I began to understand the root of my struggle. During one of our sessions, she asked me a simple question: "What would happen if you said no?" I froze. The thought of saying no to a client felt like risking everything I had worked so hard to build. But as we dug deeper, I realized that my fear of setting boundaries was tied to a deeper fear of failure. I had spent years equating my worth with my ability to meet every demand, to be everything to everyone. Saying no felt like admitting I wasn't good enough.

The first time I set a boundary with a client, it was terrifying. They had asked for a major change to a project at the last minute, and I knew it would require my team to work overtime to meet the deadline. My heart raced as I typed out an email: "I understand how important this change is to you, but we won't be able to accommodate it without adjusting the timeline. Here's what we can do instead..." I stared at the screen for what felt like hours before hitting send. My hands were shaking, and my mind was flooded with worst-case scenarios. *What if they're angry? What if they take their business elsewhere? What if this ruins my reputation?*

But none of that happened. The client responded with understanding and even thanked me for being transparent. It was a small moment, but it was a turning point for me. For the first time, I realized that setting a boundary didn't mean losing a client; it meant creating a healthier, mores sustainable way of doing business.

Over time, I started setting boundaries in other areas of my work. I stopped answering emails after 7 PM and made it clear that weekends were off-limits for non-urgent matters. I delegated tasks to my team instead of trying to do everything myself. And I learned to say no to projects that didn't align with my values or goals.

It wasn't easy. There were moments of guilt, moments of doubt, moments when I wondered if I was making the right choice. But with each boundary I set, I felt a little more in control. I realized that boundaries weren't about pushing people away; they were about creating space for the work and relationships that truly mattered.

Looking back, I can see how much I've grown. I'm no longer the business owner who says yes to everything, who sacrifices her own well-being to keep everyone else happy. I'm still learning, still stumbling, but I'm proud of the progress I've made. And I want you to know that you can make that progress too. It starts with one small step, one small boundary. You don't have to do it perfectly; you just have to start.

What Are Boundaries?

Boundaries are the limits we set to protect our physical, emotional, and mental well-being. They help us define what we're comfortable with and what we're not. Here are some common types of boundaries:

- **Physical:** Personal space and touch (e.g., "I need some alone time to recharge").

- **Emotional:** Protecting your feelings and energy (e.g., "I can't discuss this topic right now, it's too overwhelming").

- **Time:** Managing your time and commitments (e.g., "I can't work late tonight, I have prior plans").

- **Material:** Setting limits on sharing possessions or money (e.g., "I'm not comfortable lending out my car").

- **Digital:** Managing technology use and online interactions (e.g., "I won't respond to work emails after 7 PM").

Boundaries aren't about controlling others; they're about taking responsibility for your own well-being.

Why Boundaries Are Crucial

Boundaries are essential for healthy relationships and self-care. Here's why:

- **They Prevent Burnout:** Without boundaries, you risk overextending yourself and running on empty.

- **They Foster Mutual Respect:** Clear boundaries help others understand your needs and limits.

- **They Help You Prioritize:** Boundaries allow you to focus on what truly matters to you.

- **They Build Trust:** When you communicate your boundaries honestly, it creates a foundation of trust and respect.

Without boundaries, relationships can become one-sided, draining, or even toxic. Setting boundaries is an act of self-respect, and it's a skill that can be learned.

Common Challenges to Setting Boundaries

While boundaries are crucial, setting them can be incredibly difficult. Here are some common challenges and how to overcome them:

Fear of Rejection or Abandonment

- *Why It Happens:* You might worry that saying "no" will lead to rejection or criticism.

- *How to Overcome It:* Remind yourself that healthy relationships are built on mutual respect, not constant approval.

Guilt and Shame

- *Why It Happens:* Many of us are taught that putting ourselves first is selfish.

- *How to Overcome It:* Reframe boundaries as an act of self-respect, not selfishness.

Fear of Conflict

- *Why It Happens:* If you grew up avoiding conflict, setting boundaries can feel terrifying.

- *How to Overcome It:* Practice assertive communication, which allows you to express your needs clearly and respectfully.

Lack of Role Models

- *Why It Happens:* If you didn't grow up seeing healthy boundaries modeled, you might not know how to set them.

- *How to Overcome It:* Seek out examples of healthy boundaries in books, therapy, or supportive relationships.

People-Pleasing Tendencies

- *Why It Happens:* Saying "no" can feel like a betrayal if you're used to prioritizing others' comfort.

- *How to Overcome It:* Practice saying "no" in low-stakes situations to build your confidence.

By understanding these challenges, you can approach boundary-setting with more compassion and clarity.

Psychological Insights

Boundaries are rooted in psychological principles that explain why they're so important:

- **Attachment Theory:** Healthy boundaries help create secure, trusting relationships.

- **Family Systems Theory:** Boundaries maintain balance in family dynamics, preventing enmeshment or disconnection.

- **Assertiveness Theory:** Clear communication is key to setting and maintaining boundaries.

Understanding these frameworks can help you see boundaries not as a burden but as a tool for creating healthier, more fulfilling relationships.

Practical Exercises

Here are some actionable exercises to help you practice setting boundaries:

1. **Identify Your Limits:** Reflect on areas where you feel drained or resentful. What boundaries do you need to set?

2. **Practice Saying No:** Role-play saying "no" to a request in a kind but firm way.

3. **Write a Boundary Statement:** Create a script for communicating a boundary (e.g., "I need some quiet time after work to recharge").

4. **Visualization Exercise:** Imagine yourself setting a boundary and feeling confident and empowered.

Examples of Healing

- **Maria's Story:** Maria set boundaries with her overbearing mother, which improved their relationship and reduced her anxiety.

- **David's Story:** David learned to say "no" to extra work projects, which allowed him to spend more time with his family.

- **Lena's Story:** Lena set digital boundaries by limiting her screen time, which improved her mental health and sleep.

Hope for Change

Setting boundaries is one of the most powerful steps you can take toward healing and growth. It's not about shutting people out, it's about letting the right people in while protecting your energy and well-being.

Remember, boundaries are not walls; they are bridges. They allow you to connect with others in ways that are healthy, balanced, and fulfilling.

As you practice setting boundaries, you'll notice a shift. You'll feel less drained, more respected, and more aligned with your true self. This is your time to reclaim your space, your time, and your worth. You are worthy of relationships that uplift and honor you.

Affirmation: "I am worthy of setting boundaries that protect my well-being and nurture my relationships."

CHAPTER 3

HOW THIS BOOK WILL HELP YOU NAVIGATE FAMILY DYNAMICS

Have you ever felt like you were walking on a tightrope, balancing the expectations of your family while trying not to lose yourself? That's what navigating dysfunctional family dynamics often feels like: exhausting, precarious, and filled with self-doubt. You might find yourself stuck in cycles of conflict, guilt, or avoidance, unsure of how to break free.

I know this feeling because I've lived it. For years, I didn't realize how deeply my family dynamics were influencing my life. I struggled with relationships, questioned my self-worth, and repeated patterns that left me feeling stuck. It wasn't until I began to understand the invisible forces at play, roles, unspoken rules, and generational patterns, that I started to reclaim my life.

This book is designed to be your guide through that same journey. It's not about fixing your family or assigning blame, it's about empowering you to see clearly, take control, and create the life you deserve. Unlike other books that focus on blame or quick fixes, this book offers a compassionate, step-by-step guide to understanding your role in the family system and reclaiming your emotional freedom.

Understanding the Role of Family Dynamics

Family dynamics shape the lens through which we view the world. They influence how we communicate, resolve conflict, and show love. In dysfunctional families, these dynamics often involve unspoken rules and rigid roles that leave little room for individuality or emotional freedom. Whether you come from a traditional nuclear family, a blended family, or a chosen family, the dynamics at play can deeply influence your life.

This book will help you:

- **Identify Patterns:** Recognize the roles and behaviors that keep you stuck.

  - *Example:* Are you always the peacemaker, sacrificing your needs to avoid conflict?

- **Break Cycles:** Understand how generational patterns of dysfunction influence your life and how to break free from them.

- **Set Boundaries:** Learn to protect your emotional and mental health without severing ties unnecessarily.

- **Heal and Grow:** Gain tools to rebuild self-esteem, manage triggers, and create healthier connections.

Psychological Insights to Navigate Family Dynamics

Navigating family dynamics isn't just about awareness; it's about understanding why these patterns exist. Here are two key psychological frameworks that underpin this book:

1. Family Systems Theory

Family systems theory views the family as an interconnected unit. Each person's behavior influences the whole, creating a delicate balance. In dysfunctional families, this balance often relies on unhealthy roles or coping mechanisms, like scapegoating or emotional enmeshment.

- *Example:* In one family, the "scapegoat" child was blamed for all conflicts, while the "golden child" was praised excessively. This dynamic kept the family stuck in a cycle of blame and favoritism.

2. Attachment Theory

Our early relationships with caregivers shape how we connect with others throughout life. Insecure attachments, born from neglect, inconsistency, or overcontrol, can lead to struggles with trust, communication, and intimacy.

- *Example:* A client who grew up with an emotionally distant parent struggled to trust partners, often fearing abandonment even in healthy relationships.

By understanding these theories, you can begin to untangle the web of family dynamics and see the patterns with clarity.

How This Book is Structured

To guide you through this journey, the book is divided into six key parts, each building upon the last to help you recognize dysfunction, reclaim your sense of self, and establish a healthier future.

The sections are divided as follows:

1. **Understanding Family Dysfunction:** You'll learn what family dysfunction is, the roles we play, such as the scapegoat, golden child, and peacemaker, and how these patterns are passed down through generations.

2. **Identifying the Problem:** We'll explore the signs of dysfunction, the struggle to be heard, and how dysfunctional communication impacts your relationships and self-perception.

3. **Rebuilding Yourself:** Healing begins with reclaiming your sense of self. This section will help you rebuild self-esteem, learn how to parent yourself, and shift from a survival mindset to one of growth.

4. **Setting and Maintaining Boundaries:** Boundaries are essential for emotional freedom. This book will teach you how to define, communicate, and maintain clear, compassionate limits that protect your well-being, even in the face of resistance.

5. **Navigating Relationships:** Healing doesn't always mean cutting people off; it means learning how to engage in relationships in a way that protects your well-being. This section covers managing difficult family members, the role of forgiveness, and creating a new legacy free from dysfunction.

6. **Moving Forward:** This final section includes journaling prompts, practical exercises, and affirmations to help reinforce your growth. It provides a roadmap for long-term healing and empowers you to embrace your power to change.

Each chapter builds on the last, providing a roadmap for understanding, healing, and empowerment.

What You'll Gain from This Book

1. Awareness

The first step to transformation is awareness. You'll uncover:

- The unspoken rules that govern your family interactions.

- The roles you've been assigned and their impact on your self-perception.

- The ways family dysfunction has shaped your relationships, choices, and emotional well-being.

2. Empowerment

This book will empower you to:

- Challenge limiting beliefs and harmful patterns.

- Set boundaries that prioritize your needs and values.

- Make choices that align with your authentic self.

3. Hope

Healing is a journey, not a destination. By the end of this book, you'll have:

- A clearer vision of the life you want to create.

- Practical tools to navigate challenges with resilience.

- A renewed sense of hope that change is always possible.

Personal Reflection

For much of my life, I didn't understand the invisible forces shaping my relationships. I thought the tension, guilt, and conflict were just part of life. It wasn't until I began examining my family dynamics, seeing the roles, the unspoken rules, and the generational cycles, that I realized I could change.

The turning point came when I decided to set my first boundary. It was terrifying, and the pushback was intense. But that moment taught me something powerful: I could take control of my life without losing my sense of compassion or love for my family. When I set my first boundary with my cousin, refusing to engage in guilt-tripping, it felt like a seismic shift. At first, she resisted, but over time, our relationship became more honest and respectful.

This book is the culmination of that journey, a guide to help you navigate your own dynamics with clarity and courage.

Practical Exercises

1. Family Dynamics Worksheet

Create a list of family members and describe them:

- The role they play (e.g., leader, caretaker, critic).

- How their behavior impacts you.

- How you currently respond to them.

Reflect: What patterns do you see? Which ones feel healthy, and which ones don't?

2. Vision for Change Exercise

Write a short vision statement for how you want your family relationships to feel.

- *Example:* "I want my relationships to   feel respectful, supportive, and balanced."

3. Role Reversal Exercise

Imagine yourself in another family member's role. For example:

- If you're the peacemaker, what might it feel like to be the critic? How does this shift your perspective?

4. Boundary Scripts

Practice setting boundaries with sample scripts for common scenarios:

- *Example:* "I understand you're upset, but I can't engage in this conversation if it turns into criticism."

5. Affirmation Practice

Repeat affirmations to ground yourself in your power:

- "I am not defined by my family's dysfunction."

- "I have the strength to create relationships that align with my values."

- "I am worthy of love, respect, and kindness."

Hope for Change

Navigating family dynamics is challenging, but it's also transformative. Healing doesn't require your entire family to change, and it begins with you. Each boundary you set, each pattern you recognize, and each moment of self-reflection brings you closer to the life you deserve.

Remember, progress is more important than perfection. As you engage with this book, take comfort in knowing you're not alone. Change is possible, and your courage in facing these dynamics will lead to a future rooted in authenticity, freedom, and connection.

Let's take the next step together. In the next chapter, we'll dive deeper into understanding dysfunction, what it looks like, how it manifests, and why it's so hard to break free.

PART ONE:

Understanding Dysfunction

CHAPTER 4

WHAT IS FAMILY DYSFUNCTION?

Imagine a house where the windows are painted over, letting in no light. Inside, everything looks normal at first glance, furniture arranged neatly, the walls freshly painted. But as you live there, you start to notice the cracks in the foundation, the walls that groan under unseen weight, and the chill that no heater can ever dispel. This is what living in a dysfunctional family can feel like: functional on the surface but filled with invisible fractures that shape your every step.

Just like that house, a dysfunctional family might look normal from the outside, but living in it can leave you feeling cold, unseen, and unsteady. Family relationships are meant to be the bedrock of our lives. They should teach us how to love, communicate, and navigate the world. When they're healthy, they provide a safe haven, a place where we feel valued and secure. But when dysfunction takes root, the very people who should lift us up can become the source of our deepest wounds.

Dysfunction isn't always obvious. It doesn't have to look like shouting matches or physical violence. More often, it's subtle and insidious. It's the critical comment that leaves you doubting your worth, the unspoken expectation that your feelings don't matter, or the constant need to walk on eggshells to avoid conflict. These patterns might not leave visible scars, but their impact runs deep, shaping how you see yourself and the world around you.

Myth vs. Truth: Family Dysfunction

Family dysfunction is often misunderstood, and these misconceptions can keep us trapped in cycles of guilt, shame, or confusion. By separating myth from reality, we can better understand the true nature of dysfunction and its far-reaching effects.

Myth: Dysfunction Is Always Dramatic or Obvious

Truth: Dysfunction is often subtle and insidious. It doesn't have to involve shouting matches or physical violence. More often, it's the quiet patterns, like emotional neglect, unspoken expectations, or walking on eggshells, that leave the deepest scars. These subtle dynamics can shape how you see yourself and the world, even if they're not immediately visible.

Myth: Dysfunction Means a Lack of Love

Truth: Love and dysfunction can coexist. Many dysfunctional families deeply care for one another but lack the tools, awareness, or emotional capacity to create healthy dynamics. Recognizing this duality is key to understanding that dysfunction isn't about a lack of love but rather a lack of healthy expression and boundaries.

Myth: You Can "Fix" a Dysfunctional Family

Truth: It's not your responsibility to fix your family, nor is it always possible. Dysfunction is often rooted in generational patterns and unresolved trauma. While you can work on your own healing and set boundaries, you cannot force others to change. True change requires willingness and effort from all family members, and not everyone may be ready or able to take that step.

Defining Family Dysfunction

At its core, family dysfunction is about imbalance. It occurs when unhealthy behaviors and patterns disrupt the emotional and psychological well-being of its members. This dysfunction often stems from unresolved trauma, unmet needs, or learned behaviors passed down through generations.

It's important to note that dysfunction exists on a spectrum. It can range from subtle emotional neglect to overt abuse, but its impact is always significant. Dysfunction doesn't discriminate, and it can occur in single-parent households, blended families, LGBTQ+ families, or even chosen families. What matters is the pattern of behavior, not the structure of the family itself.

Psychological Insights: Family Systems and Attachment Theory

Family dysfunction doesn't occur in isolation. According to Family Systems Theory, families operate as interconnected units, much like ecosystems. When one part is out of balance, it affects the whole. Dysfunctional families often adapt in unhealthy ways, such as assigning roles or suppressing emotions, to maintain a fragile sense of stability.

Attachment Theory also sheds light on family dysfunction. When caregivers are inconsistent, neglectful, or overly controlling, children develop insecure attachments. These attachments shape how we view relationships, trust others, and even see ourselves, creating patterns that echo into adulthood.

For example, a child who grows up with a parent who struggles with addiction might learn to suppress their own needs to avoid conflict. This pattern of self-sacrifice can carry over into adult relationships, leaving them feeling unseen and unfulfilled.

Examples of Dysfunctional Dynamics

- **Unresolved Trauma**: A parent who experienced neglect as a child may unintentionally replicate that neglect, leaving their children feeling unseen.

- **Learned Behaviors**: A family with a history of suppressing emotions might teach its members to avoid conflict at all costs, creating a tense but silent environment.

It's important to understand that dysfunction doesn't mean a lack of love. Many dysfunctional families deeply care for one another but lack the tools or awareness to create healthy dynamics. Recognizing dysfunction is the first step toward healing.

Common Patterns and Behaviors

Family dysfunction often follows predictable patterns. While these behaviors may vary in intensity, their impact is always profound.

1. **Enmeshment**

   Boundaries are blurred, and individuality is lost. In enmeshed families, personal needs and desires are sacrificed for the sake of the group.

   - *Example*: A parent who expects their child to share every detail of their life and discourages them from forming outside relationships.

2. **Triangulation**

   Conflicts are rarely addressed directly. Instead, a third person is brought in to mediate or take sides, creating mistrust and tension.

   - *Example*: A parent who complains about one child to another, fostering division instead of resolving the issue.

3. **Role Assignments**

Family members are cast into specific roles, such as the "golden child," "scapegoat," or "peacemaker." These roles become ingrained and dictate how each person is treated.

- *Example*: A sibling who is always blamed for the family's problems, regardless of the situation.

4. **Emotional Avoidance**

Difficult conversations are avoided, and emotions are suppressed. Over time, this creates an environment where feelings are invalidated, and unresolved issues pile up.

- *Example*: A family that never acknowledges grief or loss, pretending everything is fine to avoid discomfort.

The Subtle Signs of Dysfunction

Not all dysfunction is dramatic. In fact, some of the most damaging forms of dysfunction are the quietest. These might include:

- Feeling responsible for others' emotions, as if it's your job to keep everyone happy.

- Experiencing guilt or shame when asserting your own needs.

- pervasive sense of unease, as though you're never truly safe or accepted.

These subtle signs often go unnoticed because they're so deeply ingrained in the family dynamic. But over time, they take a toll, leaving you emotionally exhausted and disconnected from yourself.

How Dysfunction Shapes Your Life

The effects of family dysfunction don't stay confined to your home; they ripple outward, influencing how you navigate the world.

1. **Self-Esteem**

   Growing up in a dysfunctional family can leave you doubting your worth. If you were constantly criticized or overlooked, you might internalize the belief that you're not enough.

   - *Example*: "I always felt like I had to earn love by being perfect. Even now, I struggle with feeling 'enough' in my relationships."

2. **Relationships**

   Dysfunctional dynamics often become a blueprint for future relationships. You might notice that you're drawn to relationships that feel familiar, even if they aren't healthy.

   - *Example*: "I found myself drawn to partners who were emotionally unavailable, just like my parent. It felt familiar, but it left me feeling lonely and unseen."

3. **Emotional Regulation**

   Living in a chaotic or repressive environment can make it difficult to process and express emotions. You might struggle with anger, anxiety, or numbness, unsure of how to cope.

   - *Example*: "I didn't realize how much I suppressed my emotions until I started therapy. I'd been numb for so long that I didn't even know how to cry."

4. **Physical Manifestations**

Chronic stress from dysfunctional dynamics can also show up in the body. Many people experience symptoms like fatigue, headaches, or even autoimmune conditions as a result of long-term stress.

- ○ *Example*: "Living in a constant state of tension left me with chronic migraines and exhaustion. It wasn't until I addressed the emotional toll that my physical symptoms began to improve."

Breaking free from these effects requires self-awareness and courage. It's not an easy journey, but it's one that leads to profound growth and healing.

Personal Reflection

For much of my life, I didn't recognize the dysfunction in my own family. Like many people, I told myself that our struggles were normal. I minimized the impact of the tension, the criticism, and the emotional voids. I convinced myself that if I just tried harder, if I could be better, quieter, or more helpful, everything would improve.

The turning point came when I stepped back and saw the patterns clearly. My family wasn't intentionally trying to hurt me, but their actions were still harmful. The hardest decision I ever made was to walk away, not out of anger or blame, but out of love for myself. It was a painful process, but it was also liberating. For the first time, I could breathe, reflect, and begin to heal.

I've learned that love and dysfunction can coexist. My family loved me, but their unresolved pain created patterns that hurt me. Recognizing this duality was key to my healing.

Practical Exercises

1. **Family Dynamics Map**

   Draw a family tree and note patterns of behavior, such as unspoken rules, recurring conflicts, or assigned roles. Reflect: What dynamics do you notice? How have they shaped you?

2. **Reflection Questions**

   ○ "What unspoken rules did your family have?"

   ○ "How did your family handle conflict or express emotions?"

3. **Affirmations for Empowerment**

   Repeat affirmations to ground yourself:

   ○ "I am not defined by my family's dysfunction."

   ○ "I have the power to create healthier relationships."

Hope for the Future

Recognizing family dysfunction is not about assigning blame, and it's about understanding the dynamics that have shaped you and making empowered choices to move forward.

Healing doesn't always mean cutting ties. For some, it's about setting boundaries, having difficult conversations, and creating new patterns together. For others, it's about stepping away to protect their well-being. Whatever path you choose, know that you are not defined by the environment you grew up in. You have the power to break free from these patterns, to heal, and to create a life that reflects who you truly are.

As the poet Rupi Kaur once wrote, *"You do not just wake up and become the butterfly. Growth is a process."* Healing from family dysfunction is a journey, but every step forward is a step toward freedom.

Before moving on to the next chapter, take a moment to reflect: What's one small step you can take today to honor your needs and begin healing? It could be as simple as journaling your feelings or setting a boundary with a family member.

This chapter is just the beginning. In the pages ahead, we'll explore how to identify the roles you've been assigned in your family, roles like the "caretaker," "the lost child," or "peacemaker." We'll also discuss how to set boundaries, rebuild self-esteem, and create healthier relationships. No matter how entrenched the dysfunction feels, change is always possible. You've already taken the first step by opening this book. Let's take the next step together.

CHAPTER 5

THE ROLES WE PLAY

Family roles are like invisible scripts handed to us at birth, etched by the needs, expectations, and unspoken rules of the people around us. Imagine being cast in a play where the script never changes. You might be the one holding everything together, the dependable "responsible one." Or perhaps you're the family's scapegoat, shouldering blame for things that were never your fault. These roles, while offering a semblance of stability in chaos, come with a cost: your individuality, your emotional growth, and, often, your sense of self.

I vividly remember being cast as the peacemaker in my family. From a young age, I felt responsible for smoothing over arguments, keeping the peace, and making sure everyone was okay. It seemed noble at the time, like I was fulfilling an important role, but beneath the surface, I was slowly losing touch with my own needs, emotions, and sense of self. My identity became tied to soothing others, leaving little room for my own voice.

But as I grew older, something shifted. I started to express my own feelings, form my own opinions, and step outside the expectations that had been placed on me. I no longer swallowed my discomfort to maintain harmony. I questioned things, I spoke up, and for the first time, I prioritized what I thought and felt.

That's when the narrative around me changed. I was no longer seen as the helpful mediator. Instead, I became the scapegoat, the troublemaker, the one who was "causing problems." My attempts to be honest and assert my needs were met with resistance as if my refusal to play my old role was an act of betrayal. I realized then that peace had only been expected of me as long as it served others, not when it served me.

That experience taught me an important truth: family roles are not about who you are, but about what the family system needs you to be. And when you stop playing along, the system fights to keep you in place.

The truth is, these roles are not who you are. They are survival mechanisms, born out of dysfunction, designed to help the family maintain balance. But survival is not the same as living. Recognizing these roles is the first step to breaking free from their grip and reclaiming your true identity.

Understanding Family Roles

Roles in dysfunctional families are not chosen; they are assigned, often unconsciously. These roles evolve as families adapt to trauma, unmet needs, and chaos. While they may bring order, they often become cages, stifling individuality and emotional expression.

The Roles We Play:
The Golden Child

- **Scenario**: Picture a child whose life is an endless audition. Their every achievement, grades, trophies, and accolades are met with applause, but behind the curtain, they feel the weight of perfection. There's no room for mistakes, no space for vulnerability.

- **What They Feel**: Unrelenting pressure to succeed, coupled with an underlying fear of failure.

  - **Example**: Sarah was always praised for her academic success. To the world, she seemed perfect, but inside, she felt lonely and disconnected, her worth tied solely to her accomplishments.

- **Emotional Impact in Adulthood**: Even as an adult, Sarah felt like she had to be perfect at work and in her relationships. She struggled with anxiety and burnout, always fearing she'd disappoint others.

The Scapegoat

- **Scenario**: Imagine a teenager who challenges the family's dysfunction. Their honesty, rather than being appreciated, is met with blame. They are cast as the problem, the one who stirs the pot, even when they're pointing out the truth.

- **What They Feel**: Rejection, resentment, and a deep-seated belief that they are inherently flawed.

  - **Example**: Jason spoke out about his family's emotional neglect. Instead of being heard, he was labeled "disrespectful" and made to feel like he was the cause of every issue.

- **Emotional Impact in Adulthood**: Jason found himself in toxic friendships where he was constantly blamed for problems. He realized he was replaying his family dynamic in his adult life.

The Peacemaker

- **Scenario**: A young girl sits between her parents during an argument, desperately trying to calm them down. She believes it's her responsibility to keep the family from falling apart. Over time, this role becomes her identity.

- **What They Feel**: Exhaustion, resentment, and a loss of their own identity.

- ○ **Example**: Emily spent her childhood mediating her parents' fights. As an adult, she struggled to set boundaries, always putting others' needs ahead of her own.

The Lost Child

- **Scenario**: A quiet sibling retreats into their room, escaping the chaos by disappearing. They are the forgotten ones, fading into the background to avoid conflict or attention.

- **What They Feel**: Isolation, invisibility, and a lack of purpose.

- ○ **Example**: Michael spent hours alone, unnoticed by his family. He grew up feeling unimportant, unsure of how to connect with others.

- **Emotional Impact in Adulthood**: Michael struggled to form close relationships, feeling invisible even in his own marriage. He realized he'd carried his childhood role into adulthood.

The Mascot

- **Scenario**: At a tense family dinner, the youngest sibling cracks jokes to lighten the mood. Everyone laughs, but no one notices the pain hidden behind their cheerful facade.

- **What They Feel**: Emotional disconnection and a fear of vulnerability.

- ○ **Example**: Lisa used humor to diffuse tension in her family, but it left her struggling to express her true feelings.

When we step back and look at these roles side by side, a clear pattern emerges: each child adapts in a way that serves the family system, not their authentic self. The Golden Child carries the weight of perfection, the Scapegoat absorbs the blame, the Peacemaker sacrifices their identity for harmony, the Lost Child disappears into invisibility, and the Mascot hides pain behind laughter.

Children rarely choose these roles consciously. Instead, they develop as survival strategies, shaped by the unspoken rules of the household. Over time, the mask can become so ingrained that it follows them into adulthood, influencing how they work, love, and see themselves.

How These Roles Are Assigned

Roles in dysfunctional families often emerge based on personality, birth order, or the family's unspoken needs. For example:

- A stressed parent might assign the oldest child the golden child role to carry the family's hopes.

- An outspoken child might be labeled the scapegoat for challenging the family dynamic.

- A quiet child might retreat into the lost child role, escaping chaos by disappearing.

Roles can also shift over time. A golden child might become a scapegoat if they fail to meet expectations, or a peacemaker might adopt the mascot role to diffuse heightened tension. These shifts reinforce instability and further entrench the roles.

Cultural and Structural Diversity

Family roles can look different across cultures and family structures. For example:

- In some cultures, the eldest child is expected to take on the role of the caretaker, regardless of their own needs.

- In blended families, roles like the scapegoat or golden child might shift as new dynamics emerge.

Understanding these nuances helps us see how cultural expectations and family structures influence role assignments and dynamics.

The Emotional Impact of Roles

These roles shape your self-perception and relationships, often with lasting effects:

- **The Golden Child**: May develop perfectionism and fear of failure.

- **The Scapegoat**: Struggles with self-worth, internalizing blame.

- **The Peacemaker**: Suppresses emotions, leading to burnout.

- **The Lost Child**: Feels disconnected, lacking purpose, and belonging.

- **The Mascot**: Hides pain behind humor, avoiding vulnerability.

Recognizing the impact of these roles is crucial for breaking free and reclaiming your individuality.

Psychological Insights

Family Systems Theory explains that families function as interconnected systems. When one member adopts a role, it influences the entire family dynamic. These roles persist because they maintain a sense of balance, even if unhealthy. Recognizing this helps individuals step out of their assigned roles and disrupt the cycle.

Hope for Change

The roles you've been cast in are not who you are. They are survival mechanisms shaped by dysfunction, but they don't have to define you.

As Maya Angelou once said, "Do the best you can until you know better. Then, when you know better, do better." Recognizing your role is the first step toward doing better, for yourself and for your relationships.

Before moving on, take a moment to reflect: What's one small step you can take this week to challenge your assigned role? It could be as simple as saying "no" to a request or expressing your true feelings in a conversation.

In the next chapter ,we'll explore generational cycles of dysfunction and begin the process of reclaiming your identity. You'll learn how to step out of your assigned role and into the freedom of being your true self.

Imagine stepping off the stage, setting down the script, and walking into the freedom of your own story. You are not the role you've been playing. You are so much more.

CHAPTER 6

GENERATIONAL CYCLES OF DYSFUNCTION

Imagine a family tree. Its roots stretch deep into the soil, gnarled and tangled, holding the weight of generations past. The branches twist and turn, shaped by winds of hardship, trauma, and survival. Some branches are strong and vibrant, bearing fruit of resilience and love, while others are brittle and scarred, marked by storms of addiction, neglect, or unspoken pain. Now, imagine that you are one of those branches. You didn't plant the tree, and you didn't choose its history, yet its legacy lives in you, its sap flows through your veins, its scars etched into your skin.

This is what generational dysfunction feels like: a weight you didn't ask for, but one that shapes your life in ways you're only beginning to understand. The truth is, dysfunction rarely starts with us. The behaviors, beliefs, and patterns we struggle with today are often echoes of a past we never witnessed. But understanding where these cycles come from is the first step toward breaking them. You don't have to carry this weight forever. You can choose to plant new seeds, grow new branches, and build a healthier future.

Myths vs. Truths: Breaking Down Misconceptions About Generational Dysfunction

Before diving deeper, let's address some common myths about generational cycles of dysfunction. These misconceptions can cloud our understanding and make healing feel out of reach. By replacing myths with truths, we can approach this journey with clarity and hope.

Myth: "I'm destined to repeat the same mistakes as my parents."

Truth: While patterns of dysfunction can feel inevitable, they are not unchangeable. Awareness is the first step toward breaking the cycle. With intentional effort, therapy, and support, you can rewrite the script for yourself and future generations. You are not bound by your family's past you have the power to create a new legacy.

Myth: "If I ignore the past, it will go away."

Truth: Ignoring the past doesn't erase its impact. Unaddressed trauma and unresolved pain often resurface in unexpected ways, influencing relationships, mental health, and behavior. Acknowledging and processing the past is essential for healing.

Myth: "Breaking generational cycles is about blaming my family."

Truth: Breaking cycles isn't about assigning blame; it's about understanding. Your family members likely did the best they could with the tools and knowledge they had at the time. Healing is about recognizing harmful patterns, taking responsibility for your own growth, and creating a healthier future without judgment or resentment.

Understanding Generational Cycles of Dysfunction

Generational cycles of dysfunction are like ripples in a pond. An event, perhaps a trauma or a loss, sends out waves that extend far beyond the initial impact. These waves reach future generations, shaping how families communicate, and connect.

The Role of Trauma

Trauma lies at the heart of many generational cycles. It changes people, not just in how they see the world but in how they pass on their experiences to others. This isn't about blame; it's about understanding how survival mechanisms become family norms.

- **Emotional Trauma:** A parent who grew up feeling unloved may struggle to express affection, inadvertently creating the same emotional void for their children.

- **Behavioral Trauma:** Substance abuse, aggression, or avoidance can become learned behaviors, modeled as coping strategies for future generations.

- **Cultural and Historical Trauma:** Families impacted by systemic oppression, war, or displacement may carry unresolved grief and fear, shaping their interactions for decades.

Psychological Insights: Intergenerational Trauma and Epigenetics

Research shows that trauma can leave a biological imprint, a concept known as epigenetics. Think of epigenetics as a dimmer switch on a light. Trauma doesn't change the bulb (your DNA), but it can turn the light brighter or dimmer, affecting how your genes express themselves. This means that the stress or pain your grandparents endured could influence how your body responds to stress today, even if you've never experienced the same events.

Similarly, intergenerational trauma highlights how unprocessed grief or pain can create emotional patterns that persist across generations. Families might avoid discussing certain topics, suppress emotions, or normalize unhealthy behaviors, perpetuating cycles of dysfunction.

According to a 2019 study published in *The Journal of Trauma & Dissociation*, children of parents with untreated PTSD are three times more likely to develop anxiety or depression. This underscores the importance of addressing trauma to break these cycles.

Recognizing Patterns in Your Family

Breaking these cycles begins with recognizing them. Here are some key questions to ask yourself:

- What patterns do I see repeating across generations?

- How were emotions handled in my family?

- What unspoken rules shaped our interactions?

- Are there recurring themes like addiction, conflict, or neglect?

These questions can be painful, but they are also liberating. Recognizing the patterns is not about blaming your family; it's about understanding the dynamics so you can choose a different path.

Healing Examples

Emma's Story

Emma grew up in a family where emotions were taboo. When her mother passed away, the silence was deafening. As an adult, Emma started therapy to process her grief and learn how to express her feelings. Slowly, she began introducing open conversations with her own children, teaching them that emotions were safe and valid.

Jason's Story

Jason's father grew up in an abusive household and passed that anger onto Jason. Determined to break the cycle, Jason sought anger management classes and began practicing mindfulness. Today, he approaches conflict with empathy and patience, creating a peaceful home for his own family.

Nina's Story

Nina came from a long line of women who sacrificed their dreams for their families. She decided to break that pattern by pursuing her passion for art. Despite criticism, she stayed firm, teaching her children the importance of self-fulfillment.

Sarah's Story

Sarah grew up in a family where financial insecurity led to hoarding and constant anxiety about money. She realized the toll this fear had on her mental health and decided to work with a financial therapist. Over time, she built healthier financial habits and taught her children that security comes from planning and trust, not fear.

Carlos's Story

Carlos's family immigrated to a new country, carrying the weight of cultural displacement and economic hardship. Growing up, he felt caught between two worlds: his family's traditions and the new culture he was trying to navigate. Through therapy, Carlos learned to honor his heritage while creating a new narrative for his children, one rooted in belonging and pride.

Personal Reflection

In my family, struggle was a quiet, unspoken thing. My grandmother, the woman who raised me, carried the weight of keeping us afloat, working tirelessly, and making sure I had what I needed. But I could see the burden in her eyes, the exhaustion, the silent battles she never spoke about.

I remember walking into the kitchen and seeing her sitting there, staring down at the table, tears slipping down her face. She thought no one was watching. I didn't know what to say or how to comfort her; I only knew that seeing her cry made something in my chest tighten.

For the longest time, I hesitated to step forward, to ask what was wrong, afraid of what I might hear. But once I finally gathered the courage to go to her, to see if she was okay, she immediately wiped her face and forced a smile, as if nothing had happened. That moment stuck with me. It taught me that pain was something to be hidden, that struggle was meant to be endured in silence.

For years, I carried that same lesson. I became strong, independent, and tireless, just like she was. But I also learned that burying emotions doesn't make them disappear; it just makes them harder to release.

When I began exploring my family's history, I saw how deeply these patterns were rooted. Silence wasn't just my own; it was a legacy handed down from generations of people who didn't know how to speak their truth. Breaking that silence was terrifying. It meant confronting pain, risking rejection, and stepping into the unknown. But it also meant freedom.

Today, I speak my truth not just for me but for the generations that came before me and the ones that will follow.

Practical Exercises
Family Dynamics Map
o Draw a simple family tree, starting with your grandparents.
o Next to each person, note their role in the family (e.g., "the caretaker," "the rebel," "the peacemaker").
o Identify recurring patterns (e.g., addiction, emotional distance, over-achievement).

o Reflect on how these roles and patterns have influenced your own behavior and relationships.

Journaling Prompts

o "What patterns or behaviors in my family do I see repeated across generations?"

o "What would breaking this cycle mean for me and future generations?"

Visualization Exercise: Planting a New Legacy

o Close your eyes and imagine yourself as a gardener planting a new tree. Visualize the roots of this tree being nourished by love, understanding, and connection. Reflect on how your actions today can create a stronger foundation for future generations.

Hope for Change

Generational cycles of dysfunction are powerful, but they are not unbreakable. While these cycles can feel overwhelming, they are often accompanied by incredible resilience. Many families develop unique strengths in the face of adversity, creativity, adaptability, or a deep sense of loyalty. Recognizing these strengths can empower you to build on them as you work toward healing.

You have the strength to create a new legacy, one built on love, honesty, and connection. This work is not easy, but every step you take is a victory. You are not just breaking a cycle, you are planting seeds for a healthier future. And as you heal, you create a ripple effect that extends far beyond yourself.

Breaking generational cycles begins with a single step. Whether it's starting therapy, having an honest conversation with a loved one, or simply acknowledging the patterns you want to change, every action counts. Let this be the generation where the cycle ends. Let this be the chapter where your healing begins.

Part Two:

Identifying the Problem

CHAPTER 7

SIGNS YOU'RE IN A DYSFUNCTIONAL FAMILY

Imagine this: you're at a family gathering. The room is alive with laughter and the clinking of glasses. The smell of roasted turkey and pumpkin pie fills the air, and for a moment, everything seems perfect. But as the night wears on, a familiar tension seeps into the room. A mother's offhand remark cuts like a blade, her words laced with subtle judgment. A sibling's sarcastic joke, aimed at you, earns a few chuckles but leaves a sting that lingers. You laugh along, masking your discomfort, because that's what you've always done. Later, lying awake in bed, the words replay in your mind like a broken record.

Family dysfunction often feels like this, a quiet storm brewing beneath a facade of normalcy. It's the knot in your stomach when certain topics come up, the hesitation to speak your mind, the emotional exhaustion of constantly walking on eggshells. Recognizing these signs is the first step toward change, though it can be the hardest when they've been part of your reality for so long.

Myth vs. Truth: Challenging Misconceptions

Before diving deeper, let's address some common myths about dysfunctional families:

Myth: "Every family has issues, so mine isn't that bad."

Truth: While all families face challenges, dysfunction is characterized by persistent patterns of harm, neglect, or abuse that disrupt healthy relationships and emotional well-being.

Myth: "If I just love them enough, they'll change."

Truth: You cannot control or fix others' behavior. Healing begins with focusing on your own growth and boundaries.

Myth: "Dysfunction only happens in 'bad' families."

Truth: Dysfunction can exist in any family, regardless of socioeconomic status, culture, or appearance.

Personal Reflection

I grew up thinking my family's dynamics were normal. I remember one Thanksgiving when my uncles began arguing at the dinner table. Their voices rose, sharp and biting, while the rest of us sat frozen, unsure whether to interject or remain silent. My grandmother's attempt to diffuse the situation only added to the tension. I tried to speak up, but my words were dismissed, leaving me feeling invisible and powerless.

It wasn't until years later, during a therapy session, that I recognized this moment for what it was: a reflection of deeply ingrained dysfunction. My efforts to please everyone and avoid conflict stemmed from these early experiences. Realizing this was painful, but it was also liberating. It helped me take the first steps toward breaking the cycle.

Surface vs. Subtle Signs of Dysfunction
Surface-Level Signs

These are the obvious, hard-to-miss behaviors that signal dysfunction:

- **Frequent Conflict:** Arguments erupt over trivial issues, leaving everyone on edge.

○ *Example:* A parent lashes out when dinner isn't prepared "just right," turning a minor inconvenience into a full-blown fight.

- **Addictions or Dependencies:** Alcohol, drugs, or other destructive behaviors dominate family interactions.

  ○ *Example:* Family gatherings revolve around a parent's drinking, with everyone carefully managing their behavior to avoid an outburst.

- **Neglect or Abuse:** Emotional, physical, or financial mistreatment leaves lasting scars.

Subtle Signs

These are the quieter, often overlooked behaviors that create a toxic environment:

- **Guilt and Manipulation:** You're made to feel selfish for prioritizing your needs.

  ○ *Example:* "After all I've done for you, this is how you repay me?"

- **Unspoken Rules:** Expectations like "We don't talk about feelings" or "Never challenge Dad" govern interactions without being openly discussed.

- **Emotional Suppression:** Family members avoid vulnerability, leading to deflection or silence.

  ○ *Example:* You share something deeply personal, only to be met with a dismissive, "You'll be fine."

These subtle signs may seem insignificant, but together, they create an environment where connection and authenticity are impossible.

The Struggle to Speak and Be Heard

In dysfunctional families, communication often becomes a battle rather than abridge, a way to control, avoid, or deflect rather than connect. The struggle to express yourself in such environments is real and exhausting. Common patterns include:

Criticism Over Support

- *Scenario:* You share a personal achievement, brimming with excitement, only for a sibling to respond, "Don't mess it up this time." *Impact:* This leaves you questioning your worth and wondering if your accomplishments matter at all.

Gaslighting

- *Scenario:* You confront a family member about hurtful behavior, and they reply, "You're imagining things" or "You're too sensitive." *Impact:* Gaslighting erodes your confidence in your perceptions, making you doubt your feelings and experiences.

Stonewalling

- *Scenario:* During an argument, a family member refuses to engage or acknowledge your concerns. *Impact:* This leaves conflicts unresolved, creating lingering tension and making you feel ignored and unimportant.

Triangulation

- *Scenario:* A sibling involves you in a dispute with another family member, forcing you into the role of mediator. *Impact:* Triangulation increases conflict and leaves you feeling caught in the middle, unable to address issues directly.

These communication patterns leave lasting scars, silencing your voice and creating an environment where trust and emotional safety are hard to find.

The Emotional Toll of Dysfunction
The effects of family dysfunction extend beyond the home:

- **Chronic Anxiety:** You're always bracing for the next conflict, never able to fully relax.

- **Low Self-Worth:** You internalize the belief that your needs and feelings don't matter.

- **Difficulty Trusting Others:** Broken trust at home makes it hard to build healthy relationships elsewhere.

- **Emotional Exhaustion:** Constantly managing family dynamics leaves you drained, with little energy for self-care.

Self-Assessment Checklist
To help you identify signs of dysfunction in your own family, consider the following questions:

- Do family members frequently criticize or belittle each other?

- Are there unspoken rules about what can or cannot be discussed?

- Do you feel like you're walking on eggshells around certain family members?

- Are your needs and feelings often dismissed or ignored?

- Do family gatherings leave you feeling drained or anxious?

Practical Exercises

Reflective Journaling Prompt:

o Write about a time when you felt invalidated in your family.

□ What did you feel?

□ How did you respond?

□ What would have helped you feel sup-ported?

Family Dynamics Map:

o Draw a diagram of your family relationships. Identify roles (e.g., peace-maker, golden child), unspoken rules, and areas of tension. This visual tool can help you see patterns more clearly.

Letter to Your Younger Self:

o Write a letter to your younger self, acknowledging the pain you experienced and offering the love and support you needed but didn't receive. For example:

□ "Dear Little Me, I see how hard you tried to keep the peace. You didn't de-serve to feel invisible. You are worthy of love and respect."

Actionable Steps:

o Choose one boundary to set this week, such as declining to mediate a conflict or stepping away from a toxic conversation.

Examples of Healing

- **Sarah's Story (Emotional Suppression):**
  Sarah grew up in a family where crying was met with, "Toughen up." As an adult, she joined a support group and began practicing emotional openness with friends. Over time, she learned that her feelings were valid and taught her own children to embrace their emotions.

- **James' Story (Guilt and Manipulation):**
  James' family used guilt to control him. When he began setting boundaries, they pushed back, accusing him of being selfish. With the help of therapy, James built the confidence to prioritize his needs without guilt and created healthier relationships.

- **Lila's Story (Criticism Over Support):**
  Lila was the family's "golden child," always praised for her achievements but criticized for any misstep. By stepping back from her family's expectations and pursuing her true passions, she found fulfillment and self-worth.

- **Carlos's Story (Cultural Expectations):**
  Carlos felt torn between his family's traditional values and his own aspirations. Through therapy, he learned to honor his heritage while forging his own path, creating a balanced life for himself and his children.

Psychological Insights

Family dysfunction can be understood through Family Systems Theory, which sees families as interconnected systems. Dysfunction in one part of the system ripples outward, influencing everyone. For example, a parent's unresolved trauma might lead to anger or avoidance, which in turn affects how siblings interact.

Attachment Theory provides further insight. Dysfunctional family dynamics can disrupt secure attachment, leading to anxiety or avoidance in relationships. Understanding these psychological frameworks can help you break free from ingrained patterns and foster healthier connections.

Resilience and Strengths

While dysfunction can be painful, it often fosters resilience and unique strengths. Many individuals develop:

- **Empathy:** A deep understanding of others' pain.

- **Creativity:** Finding innovative ways to cope and thrive.

- **Determination:** A strong drive to break cycles and create a better future.

Recognizing these strengths can empower you to build on them as you work toward healing.

The Role of Therapy and Support

Healing from dysfunction often requires support. Here's how to get started:

- **Types of Therapy:** Individual, family, or group therapy can provide a safe space to process your experiences and learn new skills.

- **Finding a Therapist:** Ask for recommendations, use online directories, or contact local mental health organizations.

- **Support Groups:** Connecting with others who share similar experiences can reduce feelings of isolation and provide valuable insights.

Common Pitfalls to Avoid

Healing is a journey, and it's easy to fall into common traps. Be mindful of:

- **People-Pleasing:** Trying to fix or please others at the expense of your own well-being.

- **Isolation:** Withdrawing from support systems because of shame or fear.

- **Over-Identifying with the Past:** Letting your family's dysfunction define your identity.

Hope for Change

Acknowledging dysfunction is a courageous first step. It's not about blaming your family but about recognizing the patterns that no longer serve you. With awareness, you can begin to create a new narrative, one rooted in respect, understanding, and authenticity.

Healing doesn't happen overnight, but it starts with small, intentional changes: setting a boundary, seeking support, or simply allowing yourself to feel. Every step forward is a declaration of your worth: *I deserve peace. I deserve respect. I deserve to heal.*

You don't have to do this alone. Therapy, support groups, and tools like this book can guide you on your journey. As you heal, you not only free yourself but pave the way for future generations to live free from the weight of dysfunction.

Affirmation for Healing

"You are not defined by your family's dysfunction. You have the power to break the cycle, heal your wounds, and create a life filled with love, respect, and authenticity. Your healing matters, not just for you, but for generations to come."

CHAPTER 8

HOW DYSFUNCTION AFFECTS COMMUNICATION

Imagine sitting at a family dinner, your heart pounding as you weigh every word before it leaves your lips. Plates clink, voices rise and fall, and laughter weaves through the conversation. But beneath the surface, the air is thick with tension. You sense it in the sharp glances exchanged across the table, the hesitation in your voice when you're asked about work, and the way your sibling's joke cuts a little too close to the bone. You've learned the hard way that saying the wrong thing could mean hours of silent treatment or a barrage of criticism. This is the reality of dysfunctional communication, a constant dance on eggshells.

In a dysfunctional family, communication isn't about connection; it's about control, avoidance, and survival. Words become weapons, silences become shields, and every interaction feels like a carefully choreographed dance to avoid setting off a hidden tripwire. This chapter explores how communication patterns in dysfunctional families develop, the emotional toll they take, and the steps you can take to reclaim your voice and foster healthier interactions.

Myth and Truth: Dispelling Misconceptions About Dysfunctional Communication

Dysfunctional communication is often misunderstood, leading to feelings of guilt, shame, or helplessness. Let's debunk the top three myths and replace them with empowering truths:

Myth: "It's just how my family is. Nothing will ever change."

Truth: Change is possible, and it starts with you. Small steps like setting boundaries, practicing assertive communication, or seeking therapy can transform your relationships and emotional well-being. You can't control others, but you can change how you respond and protect your peace.

Myth: "I'm just too sensitive. It's my fault I feel this way."

Truth: Your feelings are valid. Dismissing them as "oversensitivity" is a form of gaslighting. Dysfunctional communication often invalidates emotions, but recognizing and honoring your feelings is the first step toward healing.

Myth: "If I set boundaries, I'm being selfish."

Truth: Boundaries are not selfish; they're essential for healthy relationships. They protect your emotional well-being and create space for authentic connections. Setting boundaries is an act of self-respect, not rejection.

The Patterns of Dysfunctional Communication

Families with dysfunctional communication often fall into predictable patterns. These behaviors may seem normal to those who've grown up with them, but they create barriers to genuine connection:

Gaslighting

What It Is: Manipulating someone into doubting their own perceptions or feelings.

Example: You say, "That comment really hurt me," and your parent responds, "You're being dramatic. I was just joking."

Impact: Over time, gaslighting erodes self-trust, leaving you unsure of your feelings or reality.

Criticism Over Support

What It Is: Dismissing achievements or focusing only on flaws.

Example: You share news of a promotion, and your sibling says, "Let's see how long this one lasts."

Impact: This constant negativity fosters low self-esteem and a fear of sharing your successes.

Stonewalling

What It Is: Withdrawing from conversations to avoid conflict or accountability.

Example: A family member shuts down mid-argument, refusing to speak or even make eye contact.

Impact: Issues remain unresolved, leaving emotional tension to simmer beneath the surface.

Triangulation

What It Is: Involving a third party to mediate or take sides in conflicts.

Example: A parent complains to you about your sibling instead of addressing them directly, forcing you into an uncomfortable position.

Impact: Triangulation creates mistrust and division, fracturing relationships further.

The Emotional Toll of Dysfunction

The effects of dysfunctional communication ripple through every aspect of your life:

- **Chronic Anxiety**: Anticipating criticism or conflict leaves you in a constant state of hypervigilance.

- **Low Self-Worth**: Being ignored or dismissed teaches you that your thoughts and feelings don't matter.

- **Trust Issues**: When communication is manipulative or dismissive, it's hard to trust others or yourself.

- **Emotional Exhaustion**: The mental and emotional effort required to navigate these dynamics leaves little room for self-care or growth.

- **Physical Manifestations**: The stress of dysfunctional communication can show up in headaches, fatigue, insomnia, or even chronic pain.

These patterns don't just stay within the family; they often spill into your friendships, romantic relationships, and work life, shaping how you connect with others and view yourself.

Practical Exercises for Healing

Breaking free from dysfunctional communication starts with small, intentional steps. These exercises can help you begin to reclaim your voice and build healthier interactions:

Reflective Journaling
- **Prompt**: Think of a recent family interaction that left you feeling dismissed or invalidated. What happened? How did you feel? What would you have needed in that moment to feel heard?
Additional Prompts: *What would healthy communication look like in this situation? What fears come up when you think about expressing your needs?*

Mapping Communication Patterns

- Create a diagram of your family's communication dynamics. Identify who tends to criticize, avoid, or manipulate, and note how these patterns have influenced your own communication style. **Tip**: Use circles to represent family members and arrows to show how communication flows (or doesn't flow) between them.

Role-Playing Assertive Communication

- Practice saying "no" or expressing your needs using "I" statements: *Example*: "I feel hurt when my accomplishments are minimized. I need to feel supported and valued." **Step-by-Step Guide**: Identify one small need you can express. Practice saying it in front of a mirror or with a trusted friend. Gradually work up to using these statements in real-life situations.

Setting a Small Boundary

- Choose one behavior to address this week, like refusing to engage in triangulation or redirecting critical comments. *Example*: "I think you should talk to them directly. I don't want to be in the middle."

Daily Emotional Check-In

- Spend five minutes each day identifying your emotions and journaling how they relate to recent interactions. This builds awareness and emotional regulation.

Psychological Insights

Understanding the roots of dysfunctional communication can demystify why these patterns persist and how to break them:

- **Family Systems Theory**

- Dysfunctional communication serves to maintain a family's emotional equilibrium, even when unhealthy.

- **Key Insight**: Disrupting these patterns can feel destabilizing at first, but it's a necessary step toward healthier dynamics.

- *Metaphor*: Think of a family as a mobile; when one piece moves, the whole structure shifts. Dysfunctional communication keeps the mobile stuck, even if it's unbalanced.

- **Attachment Theory**

  - Early experiences with caregivers shape how we communicate and connect. Insecure attachments often lead to avoidance or anxiety in communication.

  - **Key Insight**: Healing requires learning to express vulnerability and trust others with your emotions.

Healing Examples
- **Sarah's Story**
Sarah grew up with a father who dismissed her emotions as "over-reactions." As an adult, she struggled to express her feelings, fearing rejection. With the help of therapy, she began validating her own emotions and practicing open communication with trusted friends. Gradually, she reclaimed her voice.

- **James' Story**
James' family relied on triangulation, constantly pulling him into disputes he didn't want to mediate. He started redirecting these con-

versations, saying, "I think you should talk to them directly." This simple boundary reduced his stress and strengthened his confidence.

- **Lila's Story**

  Lila's mother often criticized her, leaving her hesitant to share her successes. In a support group, she learned to separate her worth from her mother's opinions. She began celebrating her accomplishments with friends who uplifted her, creating a healthier support system.

Personal Reflection

For years, I believed that silence was safer than speaking up. Every attempt to express my feelings was met with dismissal or criticism, leaving me to question whether my voice even mattered.

It wasn't until I stepped away from my family dynamics that I began to rediscover my ability to communicate authentically. The first time I set a boundary, I was terrified, but afterward, I felt a weight lift. Each small victory reinforced the truth: my words have value, even if not everyone is ready to hear them.

Hope for Change

You are not bound by the communication patterns you grew up with. With every small boundary you set, every assertive word you speak, and every time you validate your own feelings, you reclaim a piece of yourself.

Healing dysfunctional communication is a journey, but it's one worth taking. The tools and insights in this chapter are your starting point. As you practice these steps, you'll begin to see shifts, not only in how you communicate but in how you view yourself and the relationships you build.

This week, choose one small step to take toward healthier communication. It might be journaling about your feelings, practicing an "I" statement, or setting a boundary. Remember, every step forward is a victory.

Let this chapter remind you that your voice matters. Your feelings are valid. And you have the power to create a new narrative, one built on respect, authenticity, and connection.

CHAPTER 9

BREAKING THE SILENCE

The Weight of Unspoken Words

Silence has a way of enveloping you, wrapping itself around your thoughts and emotions like a heavy blanket, suffocating and in escapable. It feels like swallowing shards of glass, each unspoken word cutting deeper with every moment of suppression. You sit at the dinner table, forcing a smile while the weight of everything left unsaid crushes you. But the moment you finally speak, your voice raw and trembling, it's as if the air shifts, the weight loosens, and a long-buried part of you gasps for breath.

Imagine sitting at a family dinner, the sound of clinking glasses and murmured conversations filling the air. Someone makes a veiled comment about your life, the kind that stings but is masked as a joke. You glance down, biting your tongue, pretending the words didn't pierce you. Later, lying awake in bed, the comment replays in your mind, leaving an ache that refuses to fade.

This is the quiet storm of family dysfunction. It's not always shouting matches or slammed doors; it's the subtle ways your voice is stifled, your truth dismissed, and your identity lost in the silence. But silence isn't just the absence of sound; it's the absence of connection, and it leaves wounds just as deep.

The Cost of Silence

Remaining silent comes at a price. The pain of not being heard compounds over time, shaping how you see yourself and the world around you.

1. **Emotional Isolation**

   Silence creates a barrier that isolates you from others. It convinces you that no one cares and that your struggles are insignificant.

   Imagery: Picture standing in a crowded room, screaming at the top of your lungs, but no one even turns to look. Now imagine something worse, you don't even bother screaming anymore because you already know no one will listen. This is the emotional isolation that silence creates. It's the invisible wall that separates you from the world, convincing you that your voice doesn't matter.

2. **Unprocessed Pain**

   Suppressing emotions doesn't make them disappear. Instead, they fester, surfacing in unexpected ways.

   Example: You snap at a friend over something trivial or find yourself crying without understanding why. The pain you buried has nowhere else to go.

3. **Reinforcing Dysfunction**

   When no one speaks up, harmful behaviors persist. Silence protects the dysfunction, allowing it to flourish unchecked.

   Example: A parent's dismissive behavior is normalized, leaving younger family members to endure the same neglect. What was once painful becomes "just the way things are."

Myth vs. Truth: Breaking the Silence
Myth: Silence Keeps the Peace

Truth: Silence doesn't keep the peace, it perpetuates pain.

While staying quiet might avoid conflict in the short term, it often leads to resentment, emotional distance, and unresolved issues. True peace comes from honest communication, even when it's uncomfortable.

Myth: Speaking Up Will Make Things Worse

Truth: Speaking up might feel risky, but staying silent often causes more harm.

The fear of making things worse can be paralyzing, but silence allows harmful patterns to continue. When you speak your truth, you create an opportunity for change, even if the initial reaction isn't positive.

Myth: My Voice Doesn't Matter

Truth: Your voice matters more than you realize.

Dysfunctional families often teach us to minimize our feelings, but your experiences and emotions are valid. Speaking up isn't just about being heard, it's about reclaiming your power and self-worth.

Reflection Prompt:

Which of these myths have you believed? How has staying silent affected your life? What would it feel like to challenge these myths and speak your truth?

Why We Stay Silent

Breaking the silence feels like stepping into the unknown, and fear often keeps us tethered to the quiet.

- **Fear of Rejection**

  "What if they don't believe me?" "What if they leave me?" These fears are paralyzing, making silence feel safer than risking the truth. But ask yourself, who benefits from your silence? And who suffers because of it?

- **Doubts About Worth**

  Dysfunctional families teach us to minimize our feelings. You might wonder, "Am I overreacting? Is my pain even valid?" But minimizing pain doesn't erase it.

- **Survival Instincts**

  As children, silence was often a way to stay safe. Speaking up might have meant punishment or rejection, so we learned to suppress our voices. But what protected you then may now be keeping you stuck.

Practical Exercises: Finding Your Voice

Speaking up doesn't always start with a confrontation; it starts with reclaiming your voice in a way that feels safe and empowering.

1. **Journaling: Writing Your Truth**

   Begin by writing everything you've wanted to say but couldn't. Let the words flow without judgment.
   Prompt: "If I could say anything without fear, it would be..."

2. **Guided Visualization**

   Close your eyes and imagine sitting across from someone you trust. Picture yourself sharing your truth. What do you say? How does your body feel? Write down your thoughts afterward.

3. **Voice Journaling**

   If speaking up feels overwhelming, start by recording yourself. Speak your truth into your phone or a recorder, even if no one else hears it. Listen back to your words. With time, this can help you get comfortable with the sound of your own voice and prepare you for real conversations.

4. Gradual Steps

Practice expressing yourself in low-stakes situations. For instance, instead of brushing off a preference, say, "I'd like pasta for dinner tonight."

5. Family Dynamics Checklist

- Do you feel safe expressing your emotions?

- Are your achievements celebrated or minimized?

- Are conflicts resolved constructively or ignored?

Healing Examples

Emma's Story

Emma grew up in a family where vulnerability was taboo. She was told to "toughen up" whenever she cried, so she learned to bury her emotions deep inside. But when she joined a support group, she discovered that her feelings were valid. Slowly, she began to share her truth with her children, teaching them that it's okay to cry, to feel, and to be human. Today, her family is closer because of her openness, and Emma no longer carries the weight of unspoken pain.

James' Story

James was labeled "ungrateful" when he started setting boundaries. With therapy, he built confidence and learned to prioritize his needs. Over time, even his family began respecting his boundaries, creating healthier dynamics.

Nina's Story

As the "golden child," Nina felt immense pressure to succeed. Therapy helped her untangle her self-worth from her accomplishments. She now pursues her passions on her own terms, finding fulfillment and freedom.

Personal Reflection

I remember the exact moment I broke my silence. My chest felt tight, my palms damp with sweat, and my throat clenched around the words I had swallowed for years. Still, I forced them out, "I'm not okay."

The silence that followed was deafening. I had imagined relief, understanding, and maybe even comfort. Instead, I was met with defensiveness. Dismissal. Even anger. For a split second, I questioned if I had made a mistake, if maybe my silence had been the safer choice all along.

But then, something shifted. A spark of clarity, a flicker of strength I didn't know I had. For the first time, I realized that speaking up was never about them, it was about me.

I wasn't waiting for permission to exist. I wasn't seeking validation. I was reclaiming my right to be heard.

And in that moment, before anyone could twist my words, dismiss my pain, or make me feel small again, I felt it.

The weight lifting.

Not all at once. Not completely. But just enough for me to take my first real breath.

That moment wasn't perfect. It wasn't easy. And it certainly wasn't met with the response I had hoped for.

But it was mine.

And from that moment forward, I knew: I would never silence myself again.

If you're reading this and wondering if your voice matters, let me tell you: it does. Your moment might not look like mine, but it will be yours, and that's what makes it powerful.

Hope for Change

Imagine this: A future where you no longer second-guess your words. A life where your truth stands firm, and your voice is no longer a whisper lost in the noise.

Speaking up won't erase the past, but it will create a future where silence no longer defines you. One word, one sentence, one truth at a time, you are rewriting your story.

Call to Action

Let this chapter be your permission slip to start. Begin with one word, one sentence, one truth. Today, take one small step: write down one thing you've been afraid to say. Then, when you're ready, say it out loud. Your voice matters, and your truth deserves to be heard. And when that day comes, the day your voice is no longer buried, you will realize that you were never truly powerless. You were simply waiting to reclaim what was always yours.

Quote to Close

"Silence becomes cowardice when occasion demands speaking out the whole truth and acting accordingly."
~ Mahatma Gandhi

Part Three:

Rebuilding Yourself

CHAPTER 10

FROM SURVIVAL TO GROWTH

Imagine walking a tightrope. Beneath you, a swirling abyss of fear, pain, and uncertainty threatens to swallow you whole. Your hands tremble, your breath quickens, and the rope sways with every step. For years, you've balanced precariously, one step at a time, not out of choice, but necessity. The tightrope becomes your entire world, a place where survival feels like an endless fight. The wind howls in your ears, drowning out all but the voice of fear. You focus only on the rope, the next step, the next breath. But one day, you lift your gaze. There, in the distance, lies solid ground bathed in light, a life where fear no longer dictates your every move. This is the journey from survival to growth, where the tightrope fades into memory, and you step into a life of thriving.

Recognizing the Need for Change

For many, the shift from survival to growth comes after a moment of clarity. But for me, that moment arrived after a series of losses that forced me to re-evaluate everything. I had always been a survivor, navigating life's challenges as a lifelong entrepreneur. I started my first business at just seventeen years old. When I got married, I poured myself into launching a clothing line, believing it would be the next great chapter of my life.

But dysfunction followed me into my marriage. Both my husband and I came from dysfunctional families, and those dynamics seeped into our new life together. The result was two wounded adults trying to build a life while carrying the weight of unhealed trauma.

Closing my clothing line felt like a funeral for a dream I had nurtured with every ounce of passion and ambition. It wasn't just the end of a business; it was the loss of a piece of myself, a blow to my identity, and a stark reminder that control is sometimes an illusion. I remember sitting in the empty studio, the air thick with silence, surrounded by bolts of vibrant fabric that would never be transformed into the visions I had once imagined. Racks of elegant gowns and dresses stood like ghosts of possibilities that would never be realized. The weight of failure pressed down on me, not just for myself, but for everyone who had believed in me. Grief and shame became my constant companions, pulling me into a darkness I didn't yet understand. I existed on autopilot, moving through the motions of survival, but the fire that once fueled me had flickered into embers. I didn't yet realize that I wasn't just mourning a business, I was mourning the version of myself I had built around it.

The turning point didn't come right away. It took losing even more to realize how isolated I truly was. Despite all the times I had been there for others, offering them jobs, food, and even a place to live, I found myself with no one willing to do the same for me. I started to see the imbalance in my relationships, the one-sided support I had normalized as part of family loyalty.

Even more painfully, I began to recognize the toxic dynamics within my family. There was a hierarchy in place, a ringleader at the top, surrounded by "flying monkeys" who acted as enforcers, feeding off my struggles. They would swoop in, not to help, but to watch, to report back, and to revel in my hardships.

I had lived my entire life under the shadow of this dysfunction, carrying shame, guilt, and fear instilled in me since childhood. It took hitting rock bottom, closing my business, and losing everything, for me to finally see that this wasn't normal. This was dysfunction, a corrosive force that had shaped my life for too long. I realized I needed to break free, not just for my survival, but for my growth.

The Personal Reflection

Looking back, that time in my life feels like a whirlwind of pain and revelation. I had to face the harsh reality that the people I had always relied on emotionally were incapable of offering me the support I had so freely given to them. That realization was devastating, but it was also liberating.

I began to re-evaluate the depths of my relationships, recognizing that the loyalty I felt toward my family wasn't being reciprocated. When I thought about all the times I had stepped up for them and compared it to how they responded when I was in need, I knew something had to change.

The dysfunction was deeply embedded, not just in individuals, but in the entire family structure. The hierarchy, the ringleader, the guilt and shame, it all started to unravel in my mind. I had spent my life internalizing those dynamics, believing that my worth was tied to how much I could give and how much I could endure. But that wasn't true.

Rock bottom gave me clarity. Closing my clothing line forced me to confront the life I had been living and gave me the strength to start redefining myself. I realized I didn't have to stay tethered to a system that drained me. I could make a different choice, a choice to live for myself.

The Journey from Survival to Growth

The shift from survival to growth is rarely linear. For me, it involved a mix of small steps and big realizations. The first step was acknowledging the dysfunction and recognizing that I couldn't thrive while staying immersed in it. I had to set boundaries, something that felt foreign and uncomfortable at first, but became necessary for my healing.

Education played a vital role in my transformation. Returning to school not only gave me new tools and knowledge but also gave me a sense of purpose. Studying psychology helped me identify patterns I hadn't seen before, both in myself and in my family. It was as though someone had turned on a light in a room I'd lived in my whole life but never truly seen.

One concept that stood out was the idea of generational cycles. I realized that much of what I had experienced wasn't unique to me; it was part of a legacy of dysfunction passed down through my family. Understanding this didn't just help me heal; it gave me the determination to break the cycle for good.

Myth vs. Truth: Breaking Down Misconceptions About Growth

As I embarked on my journey, I encountered many misconceptions about what growth truly means. Here are three of the most common myths, and the realities that helped me move forward:

Myth: Growth means leaving everyone behind.

Truth: Growth doesn't always mean cutting people off. It's about setting boundaries, fostering healthier relationships, and sometimes redefining your connections. Some relationships may evolve, while others may end, but the goal is to create a supportive environment for your well-being.

Myth: Growth happens quickly once you decide to change.

Truth: Growth is a gradual process, often filled with setbacks and challenges. It's not a straight line but a series of small steps, moments of clarity, and occasional stumbles. Be patient with yourself.

Myth: If you're not thriving, you're failing.

Truth: Survival is not failure. It's a necessary phase that prepares you for growth. Honor where you are in your journey, and remember that even small steps forward are progress.

Practical Steps for Growth

Growth requires both introspection and action. Here are a few practices that helped me:

- **Boundary-Setting Exercise:**
  Identify one relationship in your life where boundaries are needed. Write down what you're willing to accept and what you're not. Practice communicating this boundary in a calm, assertive way. For example:
  "I value our relationship, but I need to prioritize my well-being. I can no longer [specific behavior]."

- **Reflective Journaling:**
  Write about a time when you felt unsupported or undervalued. How did it affect you? What changes can you make to ensure you're surrounded by people who uplift you? Consider questions like:

  - *What patterns do I notice in my relationships?*

  - *How can I better honor my own needs?*

- **Visualization Practice:**
  Close your eyes and imagine a future where you're thriving. Picture

yourself waking up in a peaceful home, surrounded by love and fulfillment. Let this vision guide your daily actions.

Hope for Change

Stepping off the tightrope isn't easy. It requires courage, clarity, and a willingness to let go of what no longer serves you. But with each step, the weight of survival begins to lift, replaced by the lightness of growth.

Growth is a journey, not a destination. It's about choosing yourself, your well-being, your happiness, your future, over the expectation sand dysfunctions of the past. As you heal, you'll discover a life filled with authenticity, connection, and peace.

Imagine waking up each morning no longer defined by the patterns of your past. Picture yourself thriving, surrounded by people who value and respect you. This is the life you deserve, and it begins with the courage to take that first step.

Reflection Questions

1. What does "survival mode" look like in your life?

2. Can you identify a relationship where boundaries are needed?

3. What small step can you take today to move toward growth?

CHAPTER 11

PARENTING YOURSELF

Imagine standing at the edge of a quiet lake, its surface reflecting the chaos of a stormy sky. The lake is your mind, and the storm represents the unresolved pain and unmet needs of your past. The wind howls, the rain stings your skin, and the waves churn violently, mirroring the fear, shame, and neglect you've carried for years. As the wind calms and the water stills, you begin to see your reflection, a clearer, steadier version of yourself. The ripples fade, and your reflection grows sharper and stronger. This is the essence of parenting yourself: calming the storm, nurturing your inner child, and becoming the caregiver you once needed.

Parenting yourself isn't about blaming the past or dwelling on what wasn't given to you. It's about recognizing those gaps and filling them with the love, support, and guidance you deserved but didn't receive. It's about asking yourself the hard questions, being patient with your growth, and showing up for yourself in ways others failed to.

Recognizing the Gaps

The journey to parenting yourself begins by identifying where you were left unsupported. For me, this journey started as a child. I struggled with reading, unable to grasp it effectively until the third grade. My family never seemed alarmed or took my education seriously, even when my teachers pointed out my struggles. I developed coping mechanisms like memorizing texts the night before class and reciting them to appear as though I was reading. But when my first-grade teacher noticed, she called me out, and the shame sank even deeper.

I remember reaching out to my uncle, hoping for support. Instead, his attempts to teach me to read turned into belittlement and chastisement. I cried at the kitchen table, tears falling onto the book I was desperately trying to read, while he cooked dinner and criticized me. I felt small, broken, and alone. Another time, my aunt dismissed me as "stupid" when I struggled to learn spelling words. She handed me a list of words, folded it under my pillow, and sarcastically suggested I pray for osmosis to help me remember.

These experiences didn't just teach me that I was on my own; they reinforced a belief that I wasn't capable, that my efforts didn't matter. And yet, even then, I found ways to survive. I learned to cheer myself on when no one else would. I became my own best friend, my loudest advocate, and my most loyal supporter.

A Defining Moment of Realization

As an adult, the absence of support became even more evident. I vividly remember a time at 26 years old when I booked and organized a fashion show at a local nightclub. It was my creation from start to finish; I designed the garments, coordinated the models, and produced the event. The nightclub was alive with energy: the hum of conversation, the flash of cameras, the music pulsing through the room. I stood backstage, heart racing, hoping to see familiar faces in the crowd. But as I scanned the room, I realized not a single family member had shown up.

That was the moment I understood that my success, my joy, and my sense of worth could no longer be tethered to those who refused to acknowledge me. I had spent too long waiting for validation from people who were never willing to give it. My accomplishments didn't matter to them, not because they weren't significant, but because *I* wasn't significant in their eyes. Instead of celebrating my achievements, they ignored them, as if my success somehow threatened their own. So, I let go of the expectation that my family would ever be my support system. Instead, I began seeking connections that could fill the void, building a chosen family of people who not only saw me but celebrated me, and who stood beside me in both triumph and hardship.

Reparenting Yourself

Parenting yourself is not an easy process. It requires confronting your inner child' sun met needs, healing the wounds left by others, and learning to nurture yourself with love and compassion. For me, this meant asking hard questions, like:

- Am I responding this way because of the dysfunction I experienced as a child?

- What is motivating my feelings?

- How can I show up for myself in this moment?

Each question became an opportunity to unlearn the messages I had internalized. Slowly, I began replacing criticism with encouragement, shame with understanding, and neglect with care.

One moment stands out as a milestone in reparenting myself. I faced a major setback in a business project and felt the familiar sting of self-doubt creeping in. Instead of berating myself, I paused, took a deep breath, and wrote in my journal: *"You're allowed to make mistakes. This doesn't define you. Take a break and try again tomorrow."* That small act of self-compassion felt like a lifeline, a quiet reminder that I was no longer alone in this; I had myself.

Myth vs. Truth: Breaking Down Misconceptions About Reparenting

As I embarked on my journey, I encountered many misconceptions about what reparenting truly means. Here are three of the most common myths, and the realities that helped me move forward:

Myth: Reparenting means you have to do everything on your own.

Truth: Seeking support from therapists, friends, or support groups is a crucial part of the process. You don't have to heal in isolation.

Myth: Reparenting is about blaming your parents or caregivers.

Truth: It's about taking responsibility for your own healing, regardless of who caused the pain. Blame keeps you stuck; reparenting sets you free.

Myth: Reparenting will erase all your pain.

Truth: Healing doesn't mean the pain disappears; it means you learn to carry it differently. You grow stronger, more resilient, and more compassionate toward yourself.

Practical Exercises

Growth requires both introspection and action. Here are a few practices that helped me:

- **Inner Child Letter:**
  Write a letter to your younger self. Acknowledge the pain and struggles they went through and reassure them that you are here now to protect and nurture them. Use prompts like:

o *What did you need to hear as a child?*

o *What would have made you feel safe and loved?*

o *What can you promise yourself now?*
Example: *"Dear younger me, I know you feel scared and alone right now, but I want you to know that I see you. I'm here for you, and I will protect you from now on."*

- **Daily Check-In:**
At the end of each day, ask yourself:

  o Did I honor my needs today?

  o How can I show myself more kindness tomorrow?

- **Affirmation Creation:**
Create three affirmations that address your inner child's needs. For example:

  o *"I am worthy of love and respect."*

  o *"I am proud of my progress, no matter how small."*

  o *"I am safe to express myself."*

- **Self-Soothing Practice:**
Create a list of comforting activities, like taking a warm bath, journaling, or listening to soothing music. When you feel overwhelmed, choose one activity from your list to center yourself.

Psychological Insights

Parenting yourself is deeply tied to the concept of inner child work, which involves reconnecting with the younger version of yourself that still carries the pain of unmet needs. Studies in neuroscience show that consistent self-compassion practices can reshape the brain's neural pathways. According to research published in *Frontiers in Psychology*, practicing mindfulness reduces activity in the amygdala (the brain's fear center) and increases activity in the prefrontal cortex, improving emotional regulation.

Building new habits through neuroplasticity requires repetition. By consistently showing up for yourself, whether through journaling, affirmations, or boundary-setting, you create lasting changes in how you perceive and respond to challenges.

Hope for Change

Parenting yourself is not about erasing the pain of the past; it's about transforming it. Each small act of kindness you show yourself becomes a step toward healing, a way of breaking the cycle of dysfunction.

Imagine a life where you wake up each morning knowing you are safe, loved, and supported, not because someone else provides it, but because you've learned to provide it for yourself. Picture your inner child smiling, no longer weighed down by fear or shame.

This is the life you can create. It starts with one simple promise: *I will show up for myself, no matter what.* Healing isn't about erasing the past. It's about rewriting your future, one act of love at a time.

Call to Action

Take a moment today to reflect on one unmet need from your childhood. How can you begin to meet that need for yourself? Write it down, share it with someone you trust, and take that first step toward healing. Remember, you are not alone in this journey. You have yourself, and that is enough.

CHAPTER 12

RECOGNIZING AND COMMUNICATING BOUNDARIES

Picture this: You're sitting across the table, the weight of their request pressing on your chest. Their voice is insistent, their eyes pleading. You feel the familiar tug of guilt, the knot in your stomach tightening as you weigh your options: say "yes" and sacrifice your peace, or say "no" and risk their disappointment. Deep down, you know agreeing will leave you drained, but the thought of refusing fills you with dread. You freeze, unsure of how to respond, and once again, their needs take precedence over your own.

This is the struggle of boundaries in a dysfunctional family. Boundaries, the invisible lines that define what's acceptable and what isn't, are often blurry or nonexistent in these dynamics. Without them, relationships become tangled, and emotional well-being suffers. Recognizing and communicating boundaries is not just an act of self-care; it's an act of survival and healing.

Understanding Boundaries

Boundaries are limits that protect your physical, emotional, and mental health. They define where you end and another person begins, allowing you to maintain your sense of self while interacting with others. In healthy families, boundaries are respected and flexible, adapting to the needs of each member. In dysfunctional families, boundaries are often ignored, crossed, or manipulated.

It's important to acknowledge that cultural and societal norms can influence how boundaries are perceived. In some cultures, prioritizing family over individual needs is deeply ingrained, making boundary-setting feel particularly challenging. However, setting boundaries is not inherently disrespectful or selfish; it's a necessary step toward creating balanced, respectful relationships.

Myth vs. Truth: Debunking Common Misconceptions About Boundaries

Setting boundaries can feel daunting, especially when surrounded by myths that paint them in a negative light. Let's debunk three of the most common misconceptions and replace them with empowering truths.

Myth: Setting boundaries is selfish.

Truth: Boundaries are not about shutting people out; they're about creating healthy, respectful relationships. Prioritizing your well-being allows you to show up as your best self to others. As the saying goes, "You can't pour from an empty cup."

Myth: Boundaries will ruin my relationships.

Truth: While some people may resist your boundaries at first, healthy relationships will ultimately thrive when both parties feel respected and understood. Boundaries clarify expectations and reduce resentment, creating a stronger foundation for connection.

Myth: I don't have the right to set boundaries.

Truth: Everyone has the right to set boundaries. Your needs, feelings, and well-being matter just as much as anyone else's. Setting boundaries is an act of self-respect and self-love.

Types of Boundaries:

Physical Boundaries

- Relate to personal space and physical touch. Example: Feeling uncomfortable when a family member invades your personal space but not knowing how to address it.

Emotional Boundaries

- Involve the ability to separate your feelings from others' emotions. Example: A parent expecting you to manage their happiness or taking offense when you express your own feelings.

Time Boundaries

- Protect how you spend your time and energy. Example: A sibling demanding your constant attention, leaving you no room for your own needs.

Financial Boundaries

- Define how money and resources are shared or managed. Example: A family member expecting financial support without considering your situation.

Digital Boundaries

- Protect your online space and communication. Example: A family member demanding access to your social media accounts or expecting immediate responses to texts.

Why Boundaries Are Difficult in Dysfunctional Families

In dysfunctional families, boundaries are often viewed as threats rather than tools for healthy relationships. Why?

- **Fear of Rejection**: Saying "no" can feel like risking the loss of love or acceptance.

- **Conditioning**: You may have been taught that prioritizing yourself is selfish.

- **Guilt and Manipulation**: Family members might use guilt to bypass your boundaries, framing their needs as more important than yours.

- **Lack of Practice**: If boundaries were never modeled for you, learning to set them can feel foreign and uncomfortable.

- **Childhood Trauma**: Early experiences, such as growing up in an environment where boundaries were punished or ignored, can shape your ability to assert boundaries in adulthood.

Understanding why boundaries are hard is the first step; the next is learning to recognize when they're being crossed.

Recognizing Boundary Violations

Boundary violations can be overt or subtle. Here are common examples:

- A parent reading your private messages or diary.

- A sibling pressuring you to mediate their conflicts with another family member.

- A family member dismissing your feelings as "too sensitive" or "overreacting."

Recognizing these violations allows you to take the first step toward addressing them. While it may feel overwhelming at first, remember that each small step toward clarity and self-respect is a victory. These violations may feel minor in the moment, but over time, they shape how we see ourselves. Let's walk through a common experience to show how subtle these patterns can be.

Evocative Scenario

Imagine a dinner table where every conversation revolves around one family member's struggles. Your attempts to steer the conversation toward lighter topics are ignored. You glance at the clock, contemplating an early departure, but when you mention leaving, you're accused of being "unsupportive." You stay, every moment feeling like a betrayal of your own needs, replaying the internal dialogue: "Why can't I just say no? Why do I always stay silent?"

Now, imagine the same scenario but with boundaries in place. At first, you try to redirect the conversation, but when that fails, you take a deep breath and say, "I understand this is important, but I need to leave by 8 p.m. tonight." Despite the initial pushback, you stand firm. You leave, carrying your peace and sense of self with you.

This is the power of boundaries: the ability to choose your well-being without sacrificing your compassion.

Practical Exercises

Journaling Prompts

- "What boundaries do I wish I had in place with my family?" "When have I felt my boundaries were violated, and how did I respond?"

Practice Saying No

- Write down a script for a common scenario where your boundaries are challenged. Practice saying it aloud until it feels natural.

Boundary Mapping

- Create a chart with three columns:

  ○ Current Boundaries/ Where They Need Adjustment/ Steps to Reinforce Them

Visualization Exercise

- Close your eyes and imagine a bubble surrounding you. This bubble represents your boundaries, strong, flexible, and protective. Visualize yourself stepping into this bubble and feeling safe and empowered.

Boundary Audit Tool

- Evaluate relationships in your life. Ask yourself: Where am I consistently overextending myself? Who respects my boundaries, and who doesn't? What one change can I make this week to protect my energy?

Healing Examples

1. Emma's Story:

Emma always felt responsible for her mother's happiness. After learning about emotional boundaries, she began gently redirecting her mother's emotional needs to a therapist. Though her mother resisted at first, Emma stood firm, and their relationship eventually became healthier.

2. Jason's Story:

Jason's brother frequently borrowed money without repaying it. Jason finally set a financial boundary, stating that he wouldn't lend money anymore. This led to a temporary strain, but Jason found peace in protecting his resources and his trust.

3. **Maria's Story**:

Maria grew up in a culture where family always came first. She struggle to set boundaries without feeling like she was betraying her roots. Over time, she learned to balance her cultural values with her need for self-care, finding ways to say "no" while still showing love and respect.

Psychological Insights

Boundaries are a core aspect of healthy interpersonal relationships, as described in family systems theory. They help define roles, responsibilities, and emotional space within a family system. When boundaries are absent, enmeshment, a lack of distinction between individuals, often occurs, leading to dysfunction.

Attachment theory highlights the importance of boundaries in forming secure relationships. Without them, individuals may develop anxious or avoidant attachment styles, struggling with intimacy or independence.

Neurological studies show that setting boundaries can reduce stress by activating the brain's prefrontal cortex, which governs decision-making and emotional regulation. Over time, consistent boundary-setting rewires neural pathways, helping individuals feel more in control of their lives.

Hope for Change

Imagine a life where your relationships feel balanced and respectful. A life where you can say "no" without guilt and "yes" without resentment.

Boundaries are not walls; they are bridges, creating pathways to healthier connections by protecting your emotional and mental well-being.

As you begin setting boundaries, expect resistance, especially from those who benefited from your lack of them. This is not a sign of failure but a reflection of the change you are creating. Stay firm. With each boundary you establish, you reclaim a piece of yourself.

Boundaries are an act of self-love, a declaration that your needs and feelings matter. You are not selfish for setting them; you are brave. And in your bravery, you inspire others to do the same. Every time you set a boundary, you are choosing yourself. Every 'no' to dysfunction is a 'yes' to peace. And with every act of self-respect, you are rewriting your story.

Personal Reflection

Learning to set boundaries was one of the hardest lessons of my life. I grew up in an environment where boundaries didn't exist. As a child, I learned to adapt to dysfunction, mistaking it for normalcy. When I entered my first serious relationship, the lack of boundaries followed me. I hoped for respect and kindness, but instead, I was met with abuse. I often asked not to be called names or mistreated, but my voice was ignored, and my boundaries were crossed.

For a long time, I gave in. I said "yes" to keep the peace, to avoid conflict, or to salvage a sense of quiet. But it came at a cost: my happiness, my self-esteem, and my sense of worth. It wasn't until I hit a breaking point that I realized my voice mattered.

The hardest lesson I ever had to learn was that it's okay to say "no." No to disrespect, no to manipulation, no to anything that made me feel small. I realized that those who truly cared about me would respect my boundaries. Those who didn't were not people I needed in my life.

Today, when I set a boundary and someone crosses it, I see it as a sign that they do not respect me or my well-being.

I've also learned to walk away from people who need me to be small and quiet to feel powerful. Setting boundaries is hard, but it is worth it.

Call to Action

As you reach the end of this chapter, take a moment to reflect on a boundary you need to set in your life. Write it down, practice stating it with confidence, and commit to upholding it. Boundaries are not just words; they are declarations of self-respect.

Repeat this affirmation to yourself:

"My needs matter. My boundaries are valid. I deserve respect and care."

Let these words anchor you as you take the courageous step of asserting your boundaries. Remember, boundaries are not walls meant to shut people out; they are doors that allow respect, love, and mutual care to flow freely.

You are not alone in this journey. For further guidance, consider reading *Set Boundaries, Find Peace* by Nedra Glover Tawwab or tuning into the *Therapy Chat* podcast for expert insights on fostering healthy relationships.

And above all, remember this: **Those who genuinely care about you will respect your boundaries. Those who don't were never truly invested in your well-being.**

Part Four:

Setting and Maintaining Boundaries

CHAPTER 13

MAINTAINING BOUNDARIES OVER TIME

Setting boundaries is a powerful first step, but maintaining them over time is where the real challenge lies. Life, relationships, and circumstances will test your resolve. Maintaining boundaries requires consistency, self-accountability, and an unwavering commitment to your own well-being. Think of it like maintaining physical health, just as you wouldn't stop exercising after one workout, boundaries require ongoing effort. This chapter will guide you through strategies to uphold the boundaries you've established, even when it's uncomfortable or difficult. By staying consistent, you'll reap emotional rewards like increased self-confidence, healthier relationships, and reduced stress.

Why Maintaining Boundaries Matters

Boundaries are not one-time declarations; they are ongoing commitments to yourself. Boundaries are like tending a garden. They require consistent care, pruning, and protection to thrive. When you maintain boundaries, you reinforce your self-worth, show others how to treat you, and create a foundation for healthier relationships. Letting boundaries slip sends the message that they aren't important, which can lead to resentment, frustration, and a loss of self-respect. Over time, maintaining boundaries not only benefits you but also models healthy behavior for others, creating a ripple effect of respect and understanding.

Callout Box: Benefits of Maintaining Boundaries

- **Self-Respect:** You honor your own needs and values.

- **Healthier Relationships:** Clear boundaries foster mutual respect.

- **Emotional Freedom:** You create space for peace and joy.

Personal Reflection: The Hardest Boundary I Ever Set

One of the hardest boundaries I ever set was with my immediate family. Walking away wasn't just about cutting ties; it was about breaking free from a cycle that had suffocated me for far too long. I made the painful yet necessary decision to end communication permanently, knowing deep down that if I stayed, I would continue losing pieces of myself.

I remember the first holiday season after I cut ties with my family. The silence was deafening. I sat alone in my apartment, staring at the twinkling lights of my Christmas tree, tears streaming down my face. The guilt was overwhelming. I felt like I had abandoned them. But then I reminded myself of the years I had spent shrinking myself to fit into their expectations. I picked up my journal and wrote, *"This pain is temporary. My peace is worth it."* Over time, the loneliness faded, and I began to build new traditions with friends who truly saw and valued me.

That boundary became the doorway to a life where I was no longer merely surviving. I was thriving. It allowed me to build relationships with people who saw me, respected me, and genuinely wanted the best for me. It helped me reclaim my voice, my worth, and my sense of self.

The experience taught me a powerful truth: setting boundaries is not an act of selfishness; it is an act of self-respect. It is not about pushing people away; it is about making room for the life, the love, and the peace you deserve.

Psychological Insights: Why We Struggle to Maintain Boundaries

The difficulty in maintaining boundaries is deeply rooted in our psychological conditioning, social upbringing, and emotional patterns. Understanding these factors can help us break free from self-sabotage and commit to our personal growth.

1. **The Fear of Rejection and Abandonment**

   Many of us were raised to believe that love is conditional, if we set limits, we risk losing relationships. The truth is, that genuine connections respect boundaries. If someone cannot handle your boundaries, it reflects their limitations, not your worth.

2. **The Need for External Validation**

   People-pleasers struggle with maintaining boundaries because they seek approval from others. Learning to validate yourself internally, rather than relying on external affirmation, fosters self-confidence and emotional resilience.

3. **The Habit of Self-Sacrifice**

   Many people, especially those raised in dysfunctional environments, are conditioned to put others' needs first. Shifting this mindset means realizing that prioritizing yourself is not selfish, it is necessary.

4. **Guilt as a Manipulative Force**

   Some individuals will use guilt as a weapon to make you question your decisions. Recognizing guilt as a manipulation tactic allows you to stand firm in your decisions without self-doubt.

5. **The Brain's Resistance to Change**
   The brain prefers familiarity, even if it is toxic, because it perceives change as a threat. Acknowledge that discomfort is a sign of growth, not an indication that you are doing something wrong.

Common Challenges to Maintaining Boundaries

Maintaining boundaries is rarely easy. Here are some common challenges and strategies to overcome them:

Guilt: Feeling selfish or mean for enforcing boundaries.

- **Strategy:** Reframe guilt as self-care, an act of protecting your peace.

- **Exercise:** Write down three reasons why your boundary is valid.

Pushback: Family members testing or outright rejecting your boundaries.

- **Strategy:** Reinforce your boundary with calm firmness.

- **Exercise:** Practice a mantra like, *"I don't need to explain myself."*

Emotional Fatigue: The effort of repeatedly standing your ground.

- **Strategy:** Recognize this fatigue and prepare for future moments of weakness.

- **Exercise:** List three ways to recharge when you feel drained.

Loneliness: Losing relationships that cannot adapt to your boundaries.

- **Strategy:** Focus on building new, supportive connections.

Self-Doubt: Wondering if you're being too rigid or unfair.

- **Strategy:** Revisit your "why" and remind yourself of your values.

Fear of Conflict: Avoiding boundary-setting to keep the peace.

- **Strategy:** Practice assertive communication and remind yourself that short-term discomfort leads to long-term peace.

Strategies for Sustaining Your Boundaries

- **Revisit Your "Why"**

  Remind yourself why you set the boundary in the first place. Write it down and keep it visible if needed.

  - *Example:* "I set this boundary because I value my mental health and need to feel safe in my relationships."

- **Practice Self-Accountability**

  You are responsible for maintaining your boundaries. When you're tempted to let them slide, ask yourself:

  - *"Am I honoring my own needs?"*

  - *"What will happen if I allow this boundary to be crossed?"*

- **Reinforce with Communication**

  Consistency in communication is vital. If someone crosses your boundary, address it calmly and assertively.

  - *Example:* "I value our friendship, but I need you to respect my time by calling before visiting. Let's plan a better way to meet."

- **Build a Support System**
Surround yourself with people who respect your boundaries and uplift you. If you don't have that circle yet, focus on being your own biggest cheerleader.

- **Create Rituals to Reaffirm Your Commitment**
Develop practices that remind you to uphold your boundaries, such as journaling, meditating, or reviewing affirmations.

  ○ *Journaling Prompt:* "What boundary did I uphold today, and how did it make me feel?"

  ○ *Affirmations:* "I deserve respect," or "My boundaries protect my peace."

- **Celebrate Small Wins**
Every time you uphold a boundary, take a moment to acknowledge your progress. Celebrate your courage and resilience, no matter how small the victory feels.

Cultural and Generational Dynamics

In many cultures, setting boundaries with elders or family members is seen as disrespectful. If you grew up in such an environment, you might feel torn between honoring your roots and protecting your well-being. Remember: boundaries are not about rejecting your culture, they're about creating space for your authentic self to thrive.

Call to Action: Your Boundaries, Your Peace

Think of one boundary you've been struggling to maintain. What's one small step you can take today to reinforce it? Whether it's saying no to a request that drains you or having a calm conversation with someone who's overstepping, remember that every act of boundary-setting is a gift to your future self. Keep going, your peace is worth it.

As you strengthen your boundaries over time, you'll inevitably face moments of resistance. Not everyone will celebrate your growth, some will challenge it. But remember, their reaction is about them, not you. In the next chapter, we'll dive into handling the pushback that often comes when you start standing firm in your needs.

CHAPTER 14

MANAGING RESISTANCE AND CONFLICT FROM OTHERS

You finally do it, you say no. You take a deep breath, bracing for relief, understanding, maybe even respect. But instead, their expression darkens. Their voice sharpens. Suddenly, you're no longer the person setting a reasonable boundary, you're the problem.

"After everything I've done for you?" they snap, their words laced with accusation.

The guilt hits like a gut punch. Doubt creeps in, whispering, *Did I go too far? Was I wrong to stand up for myself?*

This is the moment so many people fear when setting boundaries: the backlash, the resistance, the crushing weight of someone else's disapproval. And yet, boundaries are one of the most powerful tools for protecting your mental and emotional well-being. So why does it feel so difficult?

Because boundaries don't just change your behavior, they challenge the expectations others have placed on you. They disrupt patterns, forcing people to confront the reality that they can no longer dictate your choices. Whether it's family, friends, or colleagues, not everyone will respect your needs or welcome the shift in dynamics.

In fact, studies show that over 60% of people struggle to set boundaries because they fear upsetting others. But here's the truth :boundaries aren't about pushing people away, they're about reclaiming your space, your peace, and your sense of self.

This chapter will help you navigate the resistance, manage the conflict, and stay grounded when your boundaries are tested. Because setting boundaries isn't just about saying no to others, it's about saying yes to yourself.

Myth vs. Truth: Debunking Common Misconceptions About Boundaries

Before we dive into managing resistance, let's address some common myths about boundaries. Many of us hesitate to set boundaries because we've been taught they're selfish, mean, or relationship-ending. But these beliefs are simply not true. Let's debunk them one by one:

Myth: Boundaries are selfish.

Truth: Boundaries are an act of self-respect, not selfishness. They allow you to honor your needs while maintaining healthy relationships. Think of it like the oxygen mask on an airplane. You can't help others if you're struggling to breathe.

Myth: Setting boundaries will ruin relationships.

Truth: Healthy relationships thrive on clear boundaries. While some people may resist at first, boundaries ultimately create mutual respect and understanding. If a relationship can't withstand your boundaries, it may not be worth keeping.

Myth: If I set boundaries, I'll be seen as mean or unkind.

Truth: Boundaries can be set with compassion and kindness. Using "I" statements and acknowledging the other person's feelings can help you communicate your needs without being harsh.

Reflection Question: Which of these myths have you believed? How can reframing these beliefs empower you to set boundaries with confidence?

Why Resistance Happens: Understanding the Roots

Resistance to boundaries often stems from discomfort with change. When you set a boundary, it challenges the dynamic that others have grown accustomed to. Some people resist because they feel they're losing control or influence over you. Others struggle because your boundaries disrupt their expectations of your role in their life.

One vivid example from my life highlights this truth. After I decided to cut off communication with a relative, they contacted someone on my Facebook friends list, an acquaintance I barely knew, to reach out to me. When I read the message, my chest tightened. I felt violated, angry, and deeply disrespected. It wasn't just the act of bypassing my boundary; it was the clear lack of regard for my autonomy.

I remember staring at the message, my hands trembling as I read the words: *"Hey, I know you're not talking to your Uncle, but they're really worried about you. They just want to make sure you're okay."* My heart raced, and I felt a wave of heat rush to my face. *How dare they?* I thought. *How dare they use someone else to get to me as if my decision didn't matter?* I wanted to scream, to lash out, but instead, I took a deep breath and reminded myself: *"This is not about me. This is about their inability to respect my choice."*

Resistance, however, is rarely about you. It's a reflection of the other person's discomfort with losing access to you or their perceived power. Understanding this dynamic helps depersonalize the resistance and allows you to stand firm.

Psychological Insights: Why Resistance Happens

Resistance often stems from deeply ingrained dynamics in relationships. Here are a few psychological concepts that explain resistance:

Resistance to boundaries is rarely about you. It's about the other person's discomfort with change. When you establish a boundary, you're disrupting patterns that others have grown accustomed to. Here's why people push back and how to handle it:

1. Power Dynamics: Boundaries Challenge Control

Some people see boundaries as a loss of influence over you. When they can no longer dictate your time, emotions, or decisions, they may respond with anger, guilt-tripping, or manipulation.

- *Example:* A controlling parent who has always made decisions for you might say, *"So now you think you're too good for your family?"* in an attempt to make you feel selfish.

How to Respond: Remind yourself that autonomy is not disrespect; it's essential for your growth. Their discomfort is their issue, not yours.

2. Cognitive Dissonance: People Struggle to Reconcile the "New You"

When you set a boundary, it forces others to adjust their mental image of you. If they've always known you as the person who says yes to everything, your "no" feels like a personal rejection, even though it's not.

- *Example:* A friend who relies on you to always be available might react with frustration when you say, *"I can't talk right now, but let's catch up later."* Their irritation doesn't mean you've done something wrong; it means they are struggling to adjust.

How to Respond: Change feels uncomfortable, but that doesn't mean it's wrong. Stay firm, and let them process their feelings on their own.

3. Guilt as a Manipulation Tactic: People May Weaponize Your Compassion

Some individuals use guilt to make you question your boundaries. This is especially common in dysfunctional families ,where self-sacrifice is expected.

- *Example:* A relative might say, *"After everything I've done for you, this is how you treat me?"* to make you feel ungrateful for setting a limit.

How to Respond: Recognize guilt-tripping for what it is, a tool to control your actions. You are **not** responsible for managing others' emotions at the expense of your own well-being.

The Emotional Impact of Resistance

Encountering resistance to boundaries can stir a complex mix of emotions: frustration, sadness, guilt, or even anger. For me, frustration is the most frequent reaction. It arises from the realization that if my voice had been heard earlier, the boundary wouldn't have been necessary. Frustration also brings physical sensations, such as tightness in the chest, a knot in the stomach, or tension in the shoulders.

I remember one particularly frustrating moment when a close friend repeatedly canceled plans at the last minute. Each time, I'd feel a pang of disappointment, but I'd brush it off, telling myself, *"It's fine. They're just busy."* But after the third cancellation, I felt a surge of anger. My chest tightened, and my hands clenched into fists. I realized I wasn't just upset about the cancellations, I was upset that I hadn't spoken up sooner. If I had set a boundary earlier, I wouldn't have felt so disrespected.

These emotions can be overwhelming, but they also provide valuable insight into what matters most to you. For instance, I've encountered situations in my business where employees or clients overstepped boundaries, assuming they could take liberties with my time or resources. When I realized this behavior was becoming a pattern, I knew I had to assert myself clearly.

In these moments, I remind myself: *"My boundaries matter because I matter."* This affirmation grounds me and reaffirms myself-worth.

Exercise: Grounding Through Emotions

When you feel overwhelmed by emotions like frustration or guilt, try this grounding exercise:

1. Take three deep breaths.

2. Place a hand on your heart.

3. Silently repeat, *"My feelings are valid, and my boundaries are necessary."*

Healing Through Boundaries: Creating Space for Growth

Boundaries are not just tools for protection; they are acts of self-love that create space for healing. Cutting off communication with my immediate family was the hardest decision I've ever made, but it was also the most liberating. For the first time, I had room to focus on myself, to parent myself, discover my voice, and set goals without the constant chatter of criticism or judgment.

I remember the day I made the decision. I sat alone in my living room, staring at my phone, my finger hovering over the "block" button. My heart ached, and tears streamed down my face. *"What if I'm making a mistake?"* I thought. *"What if I regret this?"* But deep down, I knew I couldn't keep sacrificing my peace for the sake of keeping the peace. I took a deep breath, pressed the button, and immediately felt a mix of relief and grief. It was as if a weight had been lifted, but I also felt the sting of loss.

Healing doesn't happen overnight. There were moments of doubt, sadness, and loneliness. But over time, I realized how much lighter I felt without the weight of toxic relationships. Boundaries gave me the freedom to grow into the person I've always wanted to be.

Healing Example: A friend once shared how setting boundaries with her overly critical sibling transformed their relationship. Initially, her sibling was offended, but as time passed, they began respecting her wishes. This created space for a healthier and more loving connection.

Coping with the Aftermath:

If you're struggling with guilt or loneliness after setting a boundary, try these steps:

- Journal your feelings to process them.

- Seek support from a therapist or support group.

- Remind yourself: *"I am healing, and this is part of the process."*

Compassionate Boundary-Setting: Balancing Firmness and Kindness

Setting boundaries doesn't mean being harsh or shutting people out; it means protecting your peace while still treating others with respect. You can be **firm** without being **cold**, and you can enforce boundaries without guilt.

Here's how to set boundaries with **clarity and compassion**:

1. Use "I" Statements to Express Your Needs Clearly

Instead of sounding accusatory, frame your boundary as a personal need.

- **Instead of:** *"You never listen to me."*

- **Say:** *"I feel unheard when I'm interrupted. I'd appreciate it if we could take turns speaking."*

This keeps the focus on your feelings rather than making the other person defensive.

2. Acknowledge Their Feelings Without Backpedaling

You can recognize someone's emotions *without* compromising your boundaries.

- **Example:** *"I know this is hard for you, and I understand that. But I still need to prioritize my well-being."*

- **Example:** *"I care about you, but I can't be available for every crisis."*

This shows empathy while reinforcing your stance.

3. Offer Alternatives When Possible (But Only If You Want To)

If appropriate, suggest a middle ground that respects **both** of your needs.

- **Example:** *"I can't commit to that, but I'd be happy to help in a smaller way."*

- **Example:** *"I won't be able to talk tonight, but we can check in this weekend."*

This helps maintain relationships *without* overextending yourself.

Being compassionate doesn't mean bending to keep others comfortable. It means setting boundaries in a way that is kind, clear, and firm. The people who respect you will respect your limits, those who don't were never invested in your well-being.

Boundaries in Leadership: Standing Firm with Integrity

As a business owner, I've learned that leadership requires clear boundaries. Whether it's employees testing limits, clients demanding more than agreed, or collaborators assuming too much access, maintaining boundaries is essential to running a successful business.

In one instance, an employee began arriving late and missing deadlines, assuming my leniency meant the rules didn't apply to them. I addressed the issue directly: *"Your punctuality and reliability are critical to the success of this team. If this continues, we'll need to discuss alternative solutions."* While it was uncomfortable to deliver, setting this boundary preserved the integrity of my business and reinforced expectations for everyone involved.

Leadership Insight: Standing firm as a leader isn't about being authoritarian; it's about ensuring respect and alignment with shared goals.

Creating a Circle of Support: Surround Yourself with Respect

One of the greatest benefits of boundary-setting is the clarity it provides. You begin to see who genuinely values and respects you. I now surround myself with people who uplift and encourage me. These relationships feel like safe spaces where I can be my authentic self.

For those who don't respect my boundaries, I let them go with grace. This isn't always easy, but I remind myself: *"I am my own greatest advocate, and my peace is worth protecting."*

Call to Action: Your Boundaries, Your Power

Every time you stand firm in your boundaries, you're making a statement: *"I matter, my needs matter, and my peace is worth protecting."* Resistance may test your resolve, but each experience strengthens your self-assurance. Today, take one small step toward setting a boundary. Write it down, practice expressing it, and visualize yourself standing firm. Imagine the life you could create by consistently prioritizing your well-being. Keep setting boundaries, and watch your life transform.

CHAPTER 15

THE ROLE OF FORGIVENESS

What It Is and What It's Not

Forgiveness is not about forgetting. It is about letting goof the pain and reclaiming your peace.
~ Unknown

What if the person who hurt you the most never apologizes? Can you still move on? Forgiveness is one of the most misunderstood concepts in our lives. For some, it feels like a moral obligation; for others, it is a deeply personal act of liberation. Society often frames forgiveness as a prerequisite for healing, but the reality is far more nuanced. Forgiveness does not mean forgetting, condoning, or excusing harmful actions. Instead, it is a tool for releasing yourself from the grip of resentment and reclaiming your emotional freedom.

In this chapter, we'll explore what forgiveness truly means, what it doesn't mean, and how it can transform your life. You'll learn practical steps for forgiving others and yourself, along with strategies for navigating the emotional complexities of the process. Whether you're ready to forgive or still grappling with the idea, this chapter will guide you toward peace, on your terms.

What Forgiveness Is

Forgiveness is the act of consciously deciding to let go of resentment and anger toward someone who has hurt you. It's a choice you make, not for the other person, but for yourself. At its core, forgiveness is about freeing yourself from the emotional weight of past pain so that it no longer controls your life.

Forgiveness doesn't happen overnight. It's a gradual process that requires reflection, patience, and emotional work. It's also deeply personal; your journey toward forgiveness doesn't need to align with anyone else's timeline or expectations. Whether it takes weeks, months, or even years, what matters is that you're moving toward healing in a way that feels authentic to you.

What Forgiveness Is Not

To fully understand forgiveness, it's important to clarify what it isn't:

1. **It's Not Forgetting:** Forgiveness doesn't require you to erase the pain from your memory. Instead, it allows you to move forward without being consumed by it.

2. **It's Not Reconciliation:** Forgiveness is not the same as rebuilding a relationship. Reconciliation requires trust and accountability, which may not always be possible.

3. **It's Not Condoning Harm:** Choosing to forgive does not excuse or justify the harm caused.

4. **It's Not Weakness:** Forgiveness is a powerful act of reclaiming your emotional freedom, not a sign of submission.

Affirmation: *"Forgiveness is not about changing the past; it's about freeing your future."*

Myth vs. Truth: Debunking Common Misconceptions About Forgiveness

Forgiveness is often shrouded in myths that can create confusion, guilt, or even resistance. Let's break down some of the most common misconceptions and replace them with the truth:

Myth: Forgiveness means forgetting what happened.

Truth: Forgiveness doesn't require you to erase the past or pretend the hurt never occurred. It's about acknowledging the pain and choosing not to let it control your present or future.

Myth: If you forgive, you must reconcile with the person who hurt you.

Truth: Forgiveness and reconciliation are two separate things. You can forgive someone without allowing them back into your life. Reconciliation requires trust, accountability, and mutual effort, things that aren't always possible or healthy.

Myth: Forgiveness is a sign of weakness.

Truth: Forgiveness is an act of strength and self-respect. It takes courage to release resentment and reclaim your peace, especially when the hurt runs deep.

The Emotional Impact of Forgiveness

Forgiveness, when done on your terms, can have profound emotional and physical benefits. Studies have shown that forgiveness reduces stress, improves mental health, and can even enhance physical well-being. Releasing resentment frees up emotional energy that can be redirected toward personal growth and relationships that truly matter.

However, the path to forgiveness isn't always easy. It can be emotionally draining to confront the pain caused by others. Fear of being hurt again or feeling pressure to forgive prematurely can create inner conflict. Acknowledging these challenges is an essential step in your healing journey.

Forgiveness and Boundaries

One of the most important aspects of forgiveness is understanding its relationship with boundaries. Forgiving someone doesn't mean you have to allow them back into your life. In fact, setting boundaries can be an act of self-respect and self-preservation.

For example, you might choose to forgive a toxic family member but decide to limit contact with them to protect your well-being. Or, you might forgive a former friend without rekindling the relationship. Boundaries ensure that forgiveness doesn't come at the cost of your peace.

Exercise: Write down one boundary you need to set with someone who has hurt you. How will this boundary help you move forward?

Personal Reflection: When Forgiveness Feels Impossible

Forgiving someone who shows no remorse is one of the hardest challenges I've faced. It feels horrible because who wants to forgive someone who isn't sorry? When there's no accountability or change, you know they're likely to hurt you again. That's when I realized forgiveness, in some situations, wasn't an option I was willing to extend anymore. Instead, I had to make the hard decision to set a permanent boundary.

At first, the decision felt depressing. You hope, wish, and pray that the person who has hurt you will recognize their dysfunction and finally do the right thing. But some people never do. And when they don't, the only choice left is to protect yourself. Setting that forever boundary, while painful, became my way of choosing peace over chaos.

The process wasn't easy. I wrestled with guilt, wondering if I was being too harsh or giving up too soon. I felt fear. What if they retaliated? What if I was making a mistake? But beneath those emotions was a quiet sense of relief. For the first time in years, I was putting myself first.

Eventually, the decision brought clarity. With hindsight, everything becomes so much clearer. When you're in a toxic situation, you don't always see how deeply it's harming you. But once you step away, breathe fresh air, and think freely, you realize how much power there is in removing yourself.

For me, forgiveness is possible when I see genuine remorse. It's not about words or apologies; it's about action. Genuine remorse means someone is actively working to change their dysfunction, whether by going to therapy, learning new tools, or taking responsibility for their actions. When I see those efforts, it validates their sincerity and makes forgiveness meaningful.

Not everyone seeks forgiveness, and not everyone deserves it. Some people continue their harmful ways without any desire to change. In those cases, I've learned to let go of the relationship. I'm not that person, and I refuse to carry their dysfunction with me. Letting go is how I find peace and focus on my ultimate healing.

One day, I looked in the mirror and realized I no longer carried the weight of their actions. I felt lighter, freer, and more like myself than I had in years. I realized that forgiveness wasn't about them, it was about me. And sometimes, forgiving myself was the only forgiveness I needed.

Reflective Question: What boundaries do you need to set to protect your peace? What would it feel like to forgive yourself for staying too long?

Practical Steps Toward Forgiveness

Forgiveness doesn't happen overnight. Here are practical steps to help you navigate the journey:

1. **Reflect on the Pain:** Write down the specific actions that hurt you and how they've affected your life. Gaining clarity is the first step toward healing.

2. **Separate Forgiveness from Justice:** Forgiveness doesn't mean excusing behavior or foregoing accountability. Justice can coexist with forgiveness.

3. **Develop Empathy (When Possible):** Try to understand the other person's perspective without condoning their actions. This step isn't always feasible but can help in certain situations.

4. **Practice Self-Forgiveness:** Reflect on any guilt or self-blame you're carrying. Ask yourself, *"What would I say to a friend in my shoes?"*

5. **Take Small Steps:** Start with forgiving minor offenses to build your capacity for forgiving larger ones.

Exercise: Visualize resentment as a heavy weight you've been carrying. Imagine yourself gently setting it down and walking away, lighter and freer.

Healing Examples

One client shared how forgiving her overly critical sibling transformed their relationship. Initially, her siblings were defensive and angry, but over time, they began to respect her wishes. This created space for a healthier connection.

Another individual chose to forgive a friend but not reconcile. By releasing resentment, she found peace while maintaining the boundaries necessary for her well-being.

Conclusion: Forgiveness as a Gift to Yourself

Forgiveness is not about the other person. It's about you. It's a tool for releasing the emotional weight of the past and reclaiming your peace. Whether or not you choose to forgive, the journey is yours to navigate. Set boundaries, practice self-forgiveness, and remember: forgiveness is a gift you give yourself, not a favor you grant others.

Call to Action: Take a moment to reflect on one hurt you're ready to release. What would it feel like to let it go? Write down one small step you can take today, whether it's forgiving someone, forgiving yourself, or setting a boundary, to move toward peace.

Part Five:

Navigating Relationships and Emotions

CHAPTER 16

WHEN THE DUST SETTLES

Grieving the Relationship You Never Had

There is a stillness that comes after the storm. Not the calm of peace, but the hollow quiet of an abandoned battlefield. The air still smells of gunpowder. Your hands still shake. But the war is over. And now, in this heavy silence, you meet your most unexpected enemy: grief, rising like floodwater in your chest, threatening to drown you in all the love you still carry for people who never knew how to hold it.

This is the part no one tells you about.

We speak of healing. We speak of boundaries. But we rarely speak of the mourning that comes after. Because even when someone has hurt you beyond repair, even when they crossed lines that should never have existed, you may still find yourself aching for a version of them that never was – the parent who saw you, the sibling who protected you, the love that should have been safe.

The Weight of Ambiguous Loss

This is an ambiguous loss—grief without a grave to visit. No obituary to clip. No casserole-bearing neighbors to acknowledge your pain. Just you, alone with a phantom limb that still aches for a touch that never truly nourished you. Society will call this "dwelling." Your soul knows it is sacred work.

Grief does not follow rules. It does not care if the person hurts you. It only knows that something is gone. And it demands to be felt.

You might miss the comfort of tradition. The way your mother's hands looked while making your favorite meal. The scent of your grandmother's perfume. The memory of laughing with your cousins before you understood the fractures beneath the surface. These moments were real. And your love for them does not erase the harm that came later.

Myth vs. Truth: The Lies We Carry

When grieving living relationships, our minds play cruel tricks. Here are the myths that haunt us, and the truths that can set us free:

Myth: "If I truly loved them, I'd keep trying."

Truth: Love is not a suicide pact. You can love someone and still refuse to let them destroy you.

Myth: "Grieving them means I regret my boundaries."

Truth: Your grief is not a verdict – it's a testament. It proves you cared deeply, not that you were wrong.

Myth: "Blood means I owe them endless chances."

Truth: Biology is an accident, not a contract. You owe yourself safety first.

Myth: "Letting go means the love wasn't real."

Truth: Letting go means the love was real, and you finally chose yourself anyway.

The Fantasy and the Fall

I used to press my ear to the phone like a seashell, straining to hear the ocean of their love in their voicemails. But all I ever heard was static – the white noise of their conditions. Still, I saved those messages. Still, I ached.

That is the cruelest cut of grief: how your heart keeps pumping blood to a limb the relationship severed years ago.

There were nights I sat alone, wondering if I had made the right choice. Wondering if cutting them off meant I was the problem. I missed them. I missed the idea of them. I missed the fantasy I had fought so hard to keep alive – that one day they would wake up and become the people I needed them to be.

But they never did.

And I finally realized... they never would.

The grief came quietly. It was not dramatic, but it was deep. Like standing in the rubble of a home I had tried for years to repair, bricks in hand, heart wide open, only to realize the foundation had always been cracked.

The Circles of Harm: A Grounding Exercise

Grief is a cunning shapeshifter. It will dress your wounds in golden nostalgia, make you question whether the knife was really that sharp. That is why we need proof.

Take a blank piece of paper. Draw a large circle in the center. This is you.

Around it, draw smaller circles. Each one is a hurtful moment, a betrayal, a pattern you endured. Inside them, write:

- What did they do?

- How did it make you feel?

When you're done, look at this map of your pain. Then ask yourself: If someone showed you this paper and said it happened to a child you love, would you tell them to stay?

You would not.

Fold this paper. Tuck it in your wallet. Let it be the cold water you splash on your face when guilt tries to gaslight you at 2 AM.

When the World Doesn't Understand

People will say things like:

- "But they're your family."

- "You only get one mother."

- "Life's too short for grudges."

Remember: These are not truths, they are fear dressed up as wisdom. The people who say them are often terrified of their own boundaries.

Affirmations for the Heavy Days

- I am allowed to miss people who hurt me

- My grief does not make me weak – it makes me human

- I honor my pain by refusing to pass it on

- Let them call me cold – I know the fire it took to walk away

Closing: The First Peace You Ever Earned

There will be days when the silence feels too heavy, when the memories sneak in, when you wonder if it would have been easier to stay.

But remember why you left. Remember what it cost you to remain.

Let yourself grieve. Then let yourself rise.

They will call this silence "holding a grudge." You will know it as the first peace you ever earned.

Plant your flag in this scorched earth and whisper to the wind:

JUANITA E. KELLY

This is mine now.

CHAPTER 17

MANAGING RELATIONSHIPS WITH DIFFICULT FAMILY MEMBERS

Walking the Tightrope

Imagine standing in a storm, trying to hold an umbrella while the wind threatens to rip it from your hands. Managing relationships with difficult family members can feel just like that, exhausting, unpredictable, and often leaving you drenched in emotions you didn't ask for. Even after setting boundaries and rebuilding self-esteem, you might find their behaviors unchanged or even escalating. Old wounds can resurface, leaving you drained, frustrated, or doubting your progress.

This chapter equips you with practical strategies to manage these challenging dynamics while protecting your peace. You'll learn tools to foster healthier interactions where possible and make empowered decisions about the role certain family members play in your life. Above all, this chapter will help you maintain your sense of self amidst these ongoing challenges.

Understanding Difficult Family Dynamics
The Foundation of Dysfunction

Family relationships are shaped by deeply ingrained roles, expectations, and unresolved trauma. These dynamics don't appear overnight and rarely change without deliberate effort. Understanding these patterns is the first step toward breaking free from their grip.

As we explored in Chapter 5, family roles like the Golden Child, Scapegoat, and Peacemaker often emerge as survival mechanisms in dysfunctional systems. These roles, while initially providing a sense of stability, can become cages that stifle individuality and emotional growth. In Chapter 6, we also saw how generational cycles of dysfunction perpetuate these patterns, passing down unresolved pain and unhealthy behaviors from one generation to the next.

Recognizing these roles and cycles is crucial, but it's only the beginning. The real work lies in learning how to navigate these dynamics in a way that protects your well-being and fosters healthier relationships.

Recognizing Common Behavior Patterns

In difficult family dynamics, these roles often manifest through specific behaviors that can undermine your emotional safety. Some of the most common include:

- **Criticism**: Constant fault-finding, belittling, or invalidation.

- **Guilt-Tripping**: Using emotional manipulation to control or shame you.

- **Emotional Withdrawal**: Refusing to engage or using silence as punishment.

- **Control**: Dictating your choices, relationships, or actions.

Recognizing these behaviors allows you to respond strategically rather than react emotionally. Instead of seeing them as personal attacks, you can view them as patterns shaped by their own unresolved issues, ones you are not responsible for fixing.

Reflective Exercise:

Think about a difficult family relationship in your life. What recurring behaviors do you notice? How do they impact your emotions and responses? Write down one example and reflect on how you typically react.

Personal Reflection

Family gatherings were never places of warmth for me. They were stages for performance, arenas where dysfunction played out in cycles so deeply ingrained that no one questioned them. The script never changed.

It always started with my aunt, the Martyr. Christmas was her favorite time of year, until it wasn't. She would spend a fortune on gifts, stacking them high under the tree, and carefully curating presents for each family member. But when the moment came for her to unwrap hers, her face would fall. The air would shift.

Suddenly, the celebration wasn't enough. She wasn't enough.

"No one thinks about me!" she would wail, her voice thick with resentment. "I do everything for this family, and no one does anything for me."

The rest of the family barely reacted; this was routine. My grandmother kept stirring the pot on the stove, barely looking up. My other aunt and uncles exchanged knowing glances, sighing in unison, as if this, too, was part of the holiday tradition.

But I was never allowed to simply watch. Her sadness had to be someone's fault. And more often than not, that someone was me.

"You don't even care," she would say, turning her gaze toward me, her voice shaking with accusation. "You're ungrateful. Just like the rest of them."

The words landed like a slap, though no one came to my defense. Her siblings looked on, some nodding, some murmuring their agreement, all of them feeding off the moment like a pack of wolves who had found their target.

Then came my uncle, the Critic. He never raised his voice. His weapon of choice was condescension, delivered with a smirk.

"I saw what you've been up to lately," he'd say, setting down his soda-filled glass, amusement flickering in his eyes. "All that success, huh? Must be nice to play pretend at being important."

The laughter that followed was not lighthearted. It was mocking, calculated.

And just like that, the weight of the moment shifted onto me.

I knew the rules: If you defended yourself, you were too sensitive. If you stayed silent, you were proving them right.

At first, I tried to endure it, to take it all in without showing weakness. I told myself that if I just folded into myself and shrank into the background, maybe they would move on.

But they never did.

So, I found another way to survive.

When I was younger, I started disappearing upstairs, sneaking into my grandmother's bedroom, curling up in front of the TV while the noise of dysfunction carried on below me. Upstairs was safe. Upstairs, no one was watching me, no one was waiting to strike.

As I got older, hiding wasn't enough. So, I stopped going at all.

I made plans with friends on holidays, stayed at their houses, laughed with their families, and surrounded myself with people who weren't looking for a weakness to exploit. When friends weren't an option, I would go anywhere but home.

Bars. Restaurants. My office. Even just walking the streets in the cold was better than stepping inside that house. And the more I stayed away, the more I realized something that shook me to my core:

They didn't even notice I was gone.

For years, I had told myself that I mattered to them in some way, that maybe, deep down, they saw me, even if they never defended me. But the truth was this: I was only relevant to them when I was there to be their punching bag.

And when I was no longer there, the game continued without me.

That realization could have broken me. Instead, it freed me.

I had spent so much time trying to be seen, to be understood, to be enough for them. But I was wasting my energy on people who had already decided who I was in their story, a role I never agreed to play.

One day, I returned for a holiday gathering, just to see if anything had changed. My uncle, the Critic, smirked at me across the table.

"I saw what you've been up to lately," he started. The same script, the same routine.

But this time, I didn't play along.

I turned to him, my voice steady, unapologetic.

"I'm proud of my accomplishments, and I'd prefer to focus on positive conversations."

The room went silent.

For the first time, I realized something powerful:

Peace had only been expected of me as long as it served them, not when it served me. That moment taught me the importance of setting boundaries and prioritizing my own well-being, even if it meant challenging the dynamics I'd known my entire life.

It wasn't easy, but it was necessary. And it was the first step toward reclaiming my voice and my peace.

Myth vs. Truth

Many of us hold onto myths about family relationships that keep us stuck in unhealthy patterns. Let's debunk three of the most common ones:

Myth: "If I try harder, they'll change."

Truth: You cannot control or change another person's behavior. Change must come from within them. Your energy is better spent focusing on how you respond and setting boundaries to protect your well-being.

Myth: "Family should always come first, no matter what."

Truth: While family is important, your mental and emotional health should always take priority. Staying in toxic relationships out of obligation only perpetuates harm.

Myth: "If I set boundaries, they'll reject me."

Truth: Healthy boundaries are a sign of self-respect, not rejection. If someone rejects you for enforcing boundaries, it reflects their limitations, not your worth.

Reflective Question:

Which of these myths have you believed? How can shifting to the truth empower you in your relationships?

Strategies for Managing Difficult Relationships

Here are practical tools to help you navigate challenging family dynamics while protecting your peace:

- **Set and Maintain Boundaries**

- **Be Clear**: Communicate your limits directly.
  Example: "I'm not comfortable discussing this topic during family gatherings."

- **Follow Through**: If boundaries are violated, remove yourself from the situation.

• **Practice Emotional Detachment**

- **Mantra**: "Their actions are about them, not about me."

- **Visualization Exercise**: Picture a protective shield around you, deflecting negativity.

• **Use "I" Statements**

- Express feelings without assigning blame.
  Example: "I feel hurt when my choices are criticized. I'd like to focus on positive topics."

• **Choose Your Battles**

- Save energy for significant issues. Let minor comments slide when necessary.

• **Limit Contact if Necessary**

- Reduce interactions that harm your well-being.
  Example: Shift from frequent visits to occasional texts or calls.

• **Conflict Resolution Techniques**

- Use active listening: "I hear that you're upset about [X]. Let's talk about how we can address this together."

- Reframe tense moments: "Let's take a moment to calm down and revisit this later."

Reflective Question:
Which of these strategies feels most difficult for you to implement? Why?

Grieving the Family You Wished You Had

It's okay to mourn the relationships you've hoped for but never had. Grieving these losses is part of the healing process and opens the door to building healthier connections, even outside your family.

Conclusion: Embrace Your Power to Heal

You are not powerless in difficult family dynamics. While you cannot change others, you can shift how you engage, protecting your peace while fostering meaningful improvements where possible.

Final Affirmation:
"You are not responsible for fixing your family, but you are responsible for protecting your peace. Every boundary you set, every word you speak, and every step you take toward healing is a testament to your strength. You are worthy of love, respect, and a life free from toxicity."

Reflective Question:
What is one boundary you can reinforce today that will bring you closer to emotional freedom?

CHAPTER 18

NAVIGATING TRIGGERS

The Power of Triggers

Imagine your emotions are like a river. Sometimes, the water flows calmly, but other times, a sudden storm sends waves crashing over the banks. Triggers are those storms, unexpected, overwhelming, and often tied to past experiences. But just as a river can be navigated, so too can your emotional landscape.

You're sitting in a meeting, pen poised to take notes, when your boss makes an offhand comment about your work. The words are simple enough, but suddenly, your throat tightens, your pulse quickens, and a wave of frustration and shame surges through you. It's not just their remark, it's the years of criticism from a parent, the echoes of "not good enough" that resurface in an instant.

Triggers are emotional flashbacks to moments when we felt unseen, unheard, or unsafe. They're not always loud or obvious; sometimes, they creep in subtly, through a familiar smell, a certain tone of voice, or even the absence of acknowledgment. These moments can feel destabilizing, leaving us to wonder: *Why did this affect me so much?*

The truth is that triggers hold power, but they also hold promise. They are signposts pointing to wounds that need healing and areas where we can grow. This chapter will show you how to identify your triggers, understand their origins, and develop tools to navigate them. By learning to respond with clarity instead of reacting impulsively, you can take back control of your emotional landscape.

Have you ever felt blindsided by a sudden rush of emotion? You're not alone. The journey to understanding your triggers is not about perfection; it's about progress. With each step, you'll gain the ability to navigate challenges with confidence, turning triggers from barriers into bridges toward healing. Remember: your triggers do not define you; your choices do.

Understanding Triggers
What Are Triggers?

Imagine standing in line at a coffee shop, your mind on your day ahead, when a familiar song starts playing over the speakers. Without warning, your heart races, and a lump forms in your throat. You're not just hearing the music; you're reliving a breakup from years ago. This is a trigger, a powerful emotional response tied to a past experience.

Triggers are emotional flashbacks. They take us out of the present moment and pull us into unresolved pain or unmet needs. They aren't just about what's happening now but what's being stirred within us. Whether it's a comment, a smell, or even a fleeting look, triggers act as reminders of times when we felt unsafe, unseen, or unheard.

Not all triggers are negative. Positive triggers, while less commonly discussed, also play a role in our emotional experiences. A familiar scent might evoke warm memories of a childhood home, or a kind word could bring a sense of encouragement tied to a supportive relationship. Recognizing both positive and negative triggers offers a more complete understanding of your emotional landscape.

Triggers come in various forms:

- **External Triggers**: Situations, interactions, or sensory experiences that provoke an emotional response (e.g., a tone of voice, a crowded room).

- **Internal Triggers**: Thoughts, self-criticism, or sudden memories that arise spontaneously and cause emotional reactions.

- **Micro-Triggers**: Small, subtle cues like a glance or a slight change in tone that lead to outsized emotional responses.

Psychological Insight: The Neuroscience of Triggers

Triggers are deeply rooted in the brain's wiring. When you encounter a trigger, your amygdala, the brain's emotional alarm system, sends a distress signal. This overrides your prefrontal cortex, the part of your brain responsible for logical thinking and decision-making. In that moment, your brain can't distinguish between the past and present, reacting as though the old wound is happening again.

Think of your amygdala as a smoke detector. It's sensitive and designed to alert you to danger, but it doesn't always know whether the "smoke" is from a small candle or a house fire. Your prefrontal cortex acts like the firefighter, stepping in to assess the situation, but only if it isn't overwhelmed by panic.

Triggers are reinforced by avoidance. When you avoid situations that evoke certain emotions, you strengthen the neural pathways that associate those situations with danger. Conversely, engaging with triggers in a controlled way can help rewire your brain through neuroplasticity, allowing you to respond with greater calm and resilience over time.

Impactful Myth vs. Truth

Triggers are often misunderstood, leading to shame or avoidance. Let's debunk three common myths:

Myth: "Triggers are a sign of weakness."

Truth: Triggers are a natural response to past experiences. Recognizing and addressing them is a sign of strength and self-awareness.

Myth: "Avoiding triggers will solve the problem."

Truth: Avoidance only reinforces triggers by keeping them unexamined. Facing triggers with the right tools helps you build resilience.

Myth: "Triggers only come from past trauma."

Truth: While triggers often stem from unresolved pain, they can also arise from unmet needs, cultural norms, or societal pressures.

Recognizing and Identifying Your Triggers
Recognizing Patterns

Jessica always felt uneasy during team meetings, but she couldn't pinpoint why. Her heart would race, and she'd avoid speaking up, afraid of being judged. One day, after reflecting on these reactions, she realized they stemmed from years of being silenced during family discussions. Understanding this connection helped her begin to address her fear of criticism.

Triggers, like Jessica's, rarely appear randomly; they tend to follow consistent patterns linked to specific themes, words, or behaviors. Identifying these patterns helps you anticipate triggers and prepare for them with thoughtful strategies.

Steps to Identify Patterns:

1. Reflect on recent situations that caused a strong emotional reaction.

2. Note the words, actions, or circumstances that set off these feelings.

3. Look for recurring themes, such as feelings of rejection, abandon-

ment, or loss of control.

Exercise: The Trigger Map

Creating a trigger map can help you visualize and understand your emotional responses more clearly.

Steps to Create a Trigger Map:

1. Write down a recent triggering event in the center of a page.

2. Surround it with related emotions, memories, or physical sensations you experienced.

3. Draw connections to any past experiences or recurring patterns that may influence your reactions.

4. Include trigger intensity levels (low, medium, high) to understand the depth of your responses.

5. Add coping mechanisms you've used in the past and evaluate their effectiveness.

Example Expanded Map:

- **Trigger**: Criticism from a boss.

- **Emotions**: Shame, anger.

- **Physical Sensations**: Sweaty palms, tight throat, flushed cheeks.

- **Behavior**: Avoidance of follow-up tasks, procrastination.

- **Past Memory**: Being scolded for making mistakes as a child.

- **Coping Mechanism**: Distracting with social media (ineffective).

- **Intensity Level**: Medium.

By expanding the map, you can uncover deeper layers of your responses and start planning more effective strategies.

Managing Triggers in the Moment
Grounding Techniques for Immediate Relief

When a trigger arises, grounding techniques can help you regain control and stay present.

· **5-4-3-2-1 Method**: Engage your senses to anchor yourself in the present.

- Identify five things you can see.

- Name four things you can touch.

- Acknowledge three things you can hear.

- Focus on two things you can smell.

- Notice one thing you can taste.

· **Box Breathing**: Calm your nervous system with controlled breathing.
- Inhale for four counts.

- Hold your breath for four counts.

- Exhale for four counts.

- Hold again for four counts.

· **Nature Visualization**: Imagine yourself standing bare foot in a field, with roots growing from your feet into the ground, anchoring you like a tree.

Healing Triggers at Their Root
Exploring the Source

Healing starts with understanding the connection between your triggers and past experiences.

Steps to Explore the Source:

1. Identify a Trigger: Recall a specific situation where you felt emotionally reactive.

2. Trace the Emotion: Ask yourself, "What emotion did I feel? Where have I felt this before?"

3. Uncover the Need: Reflect on what was missing in the past (e.g., validation, safety, love) that may have contributed to this sensitivity.

4. Acknowledge the Memory: Accept the role this memory has played in shaping your responses.

Exercise: Rewriting the Narrative

Your triggers are tied to the stories you tell yourself about your experiences. Rewriting these narratives helps you reshape your emotional responses.

Steps to Rewrite the Narrative:

- Identify the Old Story: Write down the internal narrative tied to a specific trigger.

  ○ Example: "I'm always ignored. What I say doesn't matter."

- Challenge the Story: Reflect on whether this narrative is entirely true.

  - Ask yourself, "Is this belief based on fact or fear? Are there times when I was heard and valued?"

- Write a New Story: Replace the old narrative with one that empowers you.

  - Example: "My voice matters. Even if not everyone listens, I deserve to speak my truth."

Hope for Change: The Journey to Healing

Healing is not linear, but it is always possible. Every time you pause, reflect, and respond thoughtfully to a trigger, you are rewiring your brain and building emotional resilience. Over time, triggers that once felt overwhelming will become manageable, and you'll find yourself responding with calm and clarity rather than fear or frustration.

Imagine yourself a year from now, navigating a situation that once felt overwhelming. Picture the calm confidence you bring to the moment, the strength you've cultivated, and the freedom you've achieved. That future is within reach. It begins with each choice you make today.

Personal Reflection: My Own Journey with Triggers

I've lost count of how many times I've heard the words:

- *"You're too much."*

- *"You're too intense."*

- *"You always have to be in control."*

- *"You make things more difficult than they need to be."*

Every time, something inside me tightens. My stomach knots, my breath shortens, and suddenly, I'm no longer in the present; I'm back there, a little girl desperate to be heard, desperate to be taken seriously, desperate for someone to see me as a person who deserved to take up space.

I've always been a woman with vision. I see things not just for what they are, but for what they could be. I pour myself into everything I do, projects, relationships, goals, and dreams. But in a world that demands women be small, accommodating, and pleasing, my ambition and intensity were seen as flaws.

For years, I believed them. I softened my edges, dimmed my light, and held back, afraid that showing up as my full self would be too much for others to handle.

Then, one day, it happened again. I was in the middle of a conversation with a friend, excited, animated, passionate, laying out a plan, when that "friend" sighed, rolled their eyes, and said, *"You always make things so difficult. Why can't you just go with the flow?"*

There it was. Again.

I felt the old wound crack open, the familiar rush of shame, the internal whisper: *See? You're too much. This is why people leave. This is why they don't support you.*

For a moment, I almost shrank again. Almost believed my intensity, my brilliance, and my drive was something to apologize for.

But then, something inside me snapped.

I looked at them, really looked at them, and for the first time, I saw it clearly:

I was not "too much."

They were just not enough.

Not enough to dream as big as I do.

Not enough to keep up with my vision.

Not enough to understand that greatness takes work, discipline, and passion.

I realized that the people who call me too much are the same ones who expect me to do everything, to take on the responsibility, fix the problems, and carry the load. They want my strength, my intelligence, my work ethic, but not the power that comes with it.

They want me to be convenient, not real.

And I am not here to be convenient.

So I sat up straighter, let the shame dissolve, and said with certainty:

"I am not difficult. I am clear. I am not too much. You're just not enough for what I'm building."

And I meant every word.

That day, I stopped shrinking. I stopped apologizing. I stopped making excuses for my resilience, my ambition, and my refusal to settle.

If I am too much for someone, that is not my burden to carry. That is not my problem to solve.

And if you are reading this, if you've ever been told you're too much, too intense, too difficult, I want you to hear me clearly:

You are not too much. They are too small.

If someone can't handle your fire, your passion, or your vision, they are simply not meant to walk beside you. Let them fall behind. Let them stay where they are. Let them remain in their small, comfortable world while you go out and build your empire.

Never apologize for being extraordinary. The world is full of people who settle for mediocrity. You were never meant to be one of them.

Embrace Your Healing Journey

Healing is not about erasing triggers but transforming your relationship with them. Each step you take to understand, manage, and heal your emotional responses is a declaration of self-respect and courage.

Think of your emotional journey as tending to a garden. Triggers are like weeds, pointing to where the soil needs care. By nurturing these areas with understanding and action, you allow new growth to flourish, creating a life filled with resilience and beauty.

Empowering Reminder

You are not alone on this journey. With each trigger that you face, each boundary you set, and each moment you choose to grow, you're rewriting your emotional story. Trust in your resilience, and know that you have the strength to create a life of peace, balance, and fulfillment.

"I am more than my triggers. I am capable of healing, growth, and creating a life that reflects my strength and courage."

Part Six:

Moving Forward

CHAPTER 19
CREATING A NEW LEGACY
The Power of Legacy

Imagine a family gathering, laughter fills the air, everyone feels seen and heard, and conversations flow with honesty and respect. The warmth in the room reflects the love and care invested in these relationships. Now, compare this to the tense, conflict-filled gatherings of the past, where criticism, manipulation, or silence dominated. The stark contrast highlights the power of legacy, the intentional choices you make today to shape a brighter, healthier future.

For years, I dreaded family holidays. The tension, the arguments, the quiet disappointments. They left me feeling drained and unseen. It wasn't until I decided to step back and ask, "What kind of relationships do I truly want?" that I realized I had the power to change the narrative. That choice marked the beginning of my new legacy.

This is a journey not just of healing but of empowerment, a chance to rewrite your story and create a ripple effect of love and respect for future generations. Breaking free from family dysfunction is one of the most challenging journeys you can embark on, but it's also one of the most rewarding. It requires courage to confront old patterns, vulnerability to create new ones, and a commitment to living intentionally.

A legacy isn't just what you leave behind; it's the life you live each day. It's the way you speak to others, the boundaries you set, and the values you embody. Every decision, no matter how small, is a brushstroke in the masterpiece of your legacy. Every choice ripples into the future, proving that healing is possible and transformation is contagious.

This chapter will guide you in envisioning and cultivating a family culture that reflects your deepest values and aspirations. You'll learn how to transform old wounds into wisdom, break the cycles of dysfunction, and model the behaviors that inspire meaningful change. As you step out of the shadow of generational cycles, you're choosing to redefine what family means.

Take a moment to ask yourself:

- What kind of legacy do I want to leave?

- How can I turn the pain of the past into a purpose for the future?

With every step forward, you reclaim your power to shape relationships rooted in love, respect, and resilience.

Understanding What a Legacy Is

A legacy isn't just what you leave behind when you're gone; it's the life you live every day. It's the choices you make, the relationships you nurture, and the values you embody. Your legacy reflects how you show up for yourself and others and the example you set for those who come after you. By intentionally shaping your legacy, you can transform the shadows of dysfunction into a legacy of light, love, and resilience.

The Three Dimensions of Legacy

- **Personal Legacy:**
  This is how you live your life and embody your values. It's about how you treat yourself, pursue your passions, and navigate your challenges.

- *Example:* Taking time to care for your mental health and showing others that prioritizing well-being is a sign of strength. *How to Apply This:* Start a daily journal to reflect on your values and track how your actions align with them.

- **Relational Legacy:**
  This is the impact you have on those around you, friends, family, colleagues, and community members. It's defined by the kindness, honesty, and empathy you bring to your connections.

- *Example:* Modeling gratitude by regularly expressing appreciation to loved ones. *How to Apply This:* Practice active listening in conversations by summarizing what the other person said before responding.

- **Generational Legacy:**
  This is the collection of beliefs, habits, and dynamics you pass down to children, nieces, nephews, or mentees. It's about planting seeds of resilience, love, and empowerment for future generations.

- *Example:* Teaching children how to set boundaries, so they grow up knowing they have a voice and the right to use it. *How to Apply This:* Share family stories that highlight resilience and growth, teaching younger generations the value of perseverance.

Personal Reflection: The Betrayal That Built Me

I used to believe that if I were strong enough, smart enough, or simply "healed enough," nothing would trigger me. That one day, I would wake up, and the things that once made my heart race, my stomach drop, and my body freeze in time would be gone. But that's not how healing works.

Some betrayals don't just hurt you. They change you. They shift the way you see people, the way you see love, and most painfully, the way you see yourself.

I was 24 years old when I made the biggest investment of my life, one that I thought was for my future, for my family, and for us. I was a young mother, ambitious, and in love. Like so many women before me, I believed that love meant trust. I believed that if I gave my all, if I worked hard, if I showed up with my whole heart, it would be enough.

I did everything.

I searched for the property. I spent hours, days, weeks, combing through listings, calling agents, and visiting neighborhoods. I envisioned the life we would build in that house, the stability, the security.

I handled every single detail. I worked with the agent and the broker to ensure the loan's approval. I found and paid for the lawyer. I coordinated the inspections. I attended the walk-throughs, made sure the paperwork was in order, and double-checked every document. I was the one who made sure this home was a reality.

And when it came time for the down payment, I gave it, my money, my hard-earned savings, because I believed in what we were building together.

I remember standing there at the signing with my heart full of hope. I was so sure this was the beginning of something beautiful.

He told me to trust him, and he said that after he signed, he would add me to the deed.

He told me everything was going to be okay.

He looked me in the eyes, knowing what he planned.

I didn't know that the moment I handed over my money, it would be considered a gift, not an investment, not a contribution, not something I had every right to.

I didn't know that while I was dreaming of our future, he and his family had been planning behind my back.

I didn't know I was being used.

And then came the day I would never forget, the day I sat in a courtroom, fighting for what I had built, only to be told that I had nothing.

Not a claim.

Not a stake.

Not a right.

His attorney argued that a portion of the down payment should be applied toward the rent I supposedly owed for the six months I had lived there, while the remainder was deemed a **gift**. Rent, despite there being **no signed lease agreement**. Legally, I was **no one** in this deal. No one but a tenant. And yet, somehow, a **tenant without a lease** was bound by an agreement that never existed. I had never felt pain like that before.

I had worked for everything. I had planned everything. I had given everything. And yet, in the eyes of the law, in the eyes of the man I had loved, in the eyes of his family, I was nothing.

The weight of that betrayal crushed me.

Because this wasn't just about money.

It wasn't just about a house.

It was about the lie.

The lie that we were building something together.

The lie that he loved me the way I had loved him.

The lie that I mattered.

I walked out of that courtroom with a reality I wasn't ready to face:

I had been used.

I had been manipulated.

I had been discarded like I was nothing more than a stepping stone for his future.

And for a long time, I let it break me. I let it define me.

I questioned everything.

How could I have been so blind?

How could I have let someone take so much from me?

How could I have trusted so deeply and been so wrong?

The shame was unbearable.

I thought about every moment I had spent working toward our home. Every sacrifice.

Every ounce of energy I had poured into building something real.

And I hated myself for believing in him.

But something inside me, the part of me that refuses to be destroyed, wouldn't let this be my ending.

Because while he may have taken my money, my time, my trust,

He would not take my power.

That betrayal taught me more than any lesson I had learned before.

I learned that trust must be earned, not blindly given.

I learned that some people will take everything you offer them and never once think to give back.

I learned that not every smile is honest, not every "I love you" is real, and not everyone who stands beside you is standing *with* you.

Most of all, I learned that I will never again be in a position where someone else gets to decide my worth.

That moment, as painful as it was, made me who I am today.

Now, when I feel the triggers creeping in, the fear of being used, the hesitation to trust, the quiet whisper that asks, *What if this happens again?*, I remind myself:

This is not then. This is now.

I am not that 24-year-old girl who thought love meant sacrifice.

I am not a woman who lets others determine what she deserves.

I am not someone's stepping stone, their backup plan, or their means to an end.

I am my own foundation.

I am my own security.

I am my own safe place.

And if you are reading this, if you are carrying the weight of betrayal in your heart, I need you to hear me:

You are not weak for trusting.

You are not foolish for believing in someone.

You are not to blame for their deception.

Your kindness is not the problem.

Their greed, their dishonesty, their lack of integrity, that is the problem.

You are not your past.

You are not the betrayals you have endured.

You are not the people who have let you down.

You are strong.

You are powerful.

And with time, patience, and love,

You will reclaim your peace.

This betrayal didn't just change me, it shaped the legacy I want to leave. A legacy of strength, self-worth, and the courage to trust again, but this time, on my own terms. It taught me that even in the face of betrayal, we have the power to rebuild, to rise, and to create something beautiful from the ashes.

Reflective Question:

What betrayals have shaped you? How can you use those experiences to build a legacy of resilience and self-love?

Legacy as a Living Tree

Think of your legacy as planting a tree. Every choice you make is like watering its roots, pruning its branches, and nurturing it to grow strong. Over time, thi stree offers shade and fruit to those who come after you. Some branches might represent values like kindness or honesty, while others might symbolize hard work or creativity. The stronger and more intentional your efforts, the sturdier and more enduring your tree becomes.

Exercise: Reflecting on Your Current Legacy

Take a moment to reflect on the legacy you're creating right now. Ask yourself:

1. What kind of legacy am I shaping through my daily actions and choices?

2. Are my behaviors and habits aligned with the values I want to pass on?

3. What small changes could I make today to better reflect the legacy I want to leave?

4. What is one small action I can take this week to align my life with the legacy I desire?

Navigating Emotional Resistance

Breaking cycles of dysfunction often brings up emotional challenges like guilt, fear of rejection, or self-doubt. These feelings are natural but can be managed with intention and self-compassion.

Strategies for Managing Emotional Resistance:

- Practice mindfulness to stay present during difficult moments.

- Use affirmations like, "I am worthy of creating a legacy rooted in love and respect."

- Seek support from trusted friends, mentors, or therapists.

Reflective Exercise:

Write a letter to your younger self, acknowledging the pain of the past and affirming your commitment to change.

Cultural Contexts and Legacy

In many cultures, legacy is tied closely to tradition and family roles. These expectations can be both grounding and restrictive. While honoring tradition has its value, creating a new legacy requires balancing respect for the past with the courage to forge a path that aligns with your authentic self.

Example:

A person raised in a culture where self-sacrifice is a virtue may need to redefine their legacy to include self-care and personal boundaries, demonstrating that prioritizing one's well-being is just as valuable as supporting others.

Reflective Question:

How can I honor my cultural heritage while creating space for healthier patterns?

Practical Example of Change

When Maria realized her family's pattern of avoiding conflict, she started holding weekly family check-ins, encouraging open communication. These small but consistent acts helped build trust and emotional safety in her home. Today, her family dynamics are defined by openness and mutual respect, a reflection of the intentional legacy she has created.

Legacy-Building Toolkit

To help you take actionable steps, here's a toolkit for building your legacy:

Daily Practices:

- Gratitude journaling.

- Mindfulness exercises like deep breathing or meditation.

Weekly Habits:

- Family check-ins or gratitude circles.

- Practicing active listening in conversations.

Monthly Reflections:

- Review progress and celebrate wins.

- Adjust goals to stay aligned with your values.

Steps to Creating a New Legacy

1. **Define Your Values:** Reflect on your core beliefs and write a legacy vision statement.

2. **Break the Cycle with Intention:** Identify old patterns and com-

mit to replacing them with healthier behaviors.

3. **Model Healthy Behaviors:** Lead by example in your relationships.

4. **Foster Open Communication:** Create safe spaces for honest conversations.

5. **Celebrate Progress:** Acknowledge and celebrate small wins along the way.

Visualization Exercise: Your New Legacy

Close your eyes and imagine a family gathering years from now. Picture the faces of those around you, full of joy, acceptance, and trust. What are they saying to one another? What values are reflected in their interactions? Now ask yourself:

- What steps did I take to make this possible?

- What lessons did I pass on to help them build this reality?

- What is one small action I can take this week to bring my vision closer to reality?

Empowering Reminder

Your legacy is not fixed, it is fluid, shaped by every decision you make. You have the power to take the lessons from your past, build on them, and create a legacy of love, resilience, and authenticity.

Affirmation:

"Every small choice I make today is a step toward building the legacy I truly desire. I am the author of my story, and it's never too late to write a new chapter."

Conclusion: Embrace Your Power to Create Change

Redefining your family legacy is not an easy task, but itis one of the most meaningful journeys you can undertake. Each time you chooses elf-awareness over blame, empathy over anger, and action over avoidance, you take a powerful step toward building the family culture you've always envisioned.

Final Metaphor:

Think of your legacy as a lighthouse. It stands tall, guiding others safely through life's storms, built on a foundation of love and resilience. Each brick you lay today, whether it's an act of forgiveness, a moment of vulnerability, or a step toward healing, contributes to this beacon of hope for generations to come.

Empowering Affirmation:

"I am the bridge between the pain of the past and the promise of the future. Each choice I make today builds a legacy of courage, compassion, and boundless love."

CHAPTER 20

JOURNALING PROMPTS FOR REFLECTION

Discovering Yourself Through Journaling

Picture this: The soft glow of a nearby lamp casts a warm light on the blank page before you. The faint scratch of pen on paper echoes in the stillness as emotions and memories find their way into words. In this quiet moment, you're not just writing; you're unraveling layers of yourself, one thought at a time.

Journaling is more than putting pen to paper. It's a journey of self-discovery, a safe space where you can explore your inner world without judgment. It invites you to confront the shadows of your past, celebrate the triumphs of your present, and imagine the possibilities of your future.

Yet, many of us hesitate to begin. We wonder if our words will make sense or fear that our thoughts are too chaotic to capture. Let go of those worries. Journaling isn't about perfect grammar or polished prose; it's about showing up authentically, as you are, and giving your inner voice a chance to be heard.

This chapter is your guide to using this powerful tool to understand the intricate dynamics of your family and begin the process of healing and growth.

The Science and Soul of Journaling

Imagine journaling as planting a garden. Each entry is a seed, carefully placed into the soil of your mind and heart. Over time, as you nurture these seeds with reflection and honesty, they grow into clarity, understanding, and personal growth.

Research has shown that this process offers profound psychological and physical benefits. Consistent journaling reduces stress, increases emotional awareness, and strengthens problem-solving abilities. It can even boost immune function and improve sleep quality. Neuroscience reveals that writing helps regulate our nervous system by externalizing our inner chaos, giving us the distance needed to process emotions and reframe experiences.

In the context of family dysfunction, journaling becomes a powerful ally. It provides a private, judgment-free zone to:

- Release pent-up emotions and uncover hidden fears.

- Untangle the emotional knots created by past experiences.

- Identify the beliefs and patterns that no longer serve you.

- Connect dots and unlock the wisdom within yourself.

It's not just about looking back; it's about moving forward with intention.

Letting Go of the Myths

Think you don't have time? Or perhaps you're worried you're "not good at writing"? Let these myths go. Journaling doesn't require hours or literary skill.

Myth: It has to be long.
Truth: Even five minutes a day has impact.

Myth: It has to be sentences.

Truth: Bullet points, incomplete thoughts, or even doodles are enough.

Myth: It will be too painful.

Truth: It gives you control over the pace of your exploration.

There's no right or wrong way, just your way.

A Reader-Centric Example:

Take Sarah, for example. She resisted journaling for years, fearing it would dredge up emotions she wasn't ready to face. But when she finally gave it a try, starting with just one sentence a day, she found that journaling became her lifeline. She uncovered childhood patterns, understood the roots of her fears, and began to rewrite her narrative. Journaling didn't change her past, but it gave her the tools to reclaim her future.

Core Practice: Journaling Prompts for Dysfunctional Families

Dysfunctional families often operate within invisible patterns, unspoken rules, and roles that shape us in ways we may not fully realize. Use the following prompts to gently explore these dynamics.

1.Family Roles: Understanding the Roles We Played

Roles like the peacemaker, scapegoat, or hero often emerge as coping mechanisms. Recognizing them is the first step to releasing those that no longer serve you.

- **Prompt:** "What role did I play in my family growing up? Was this role assigned to me, or did I take it on to cope?"

- **Prompt:** "What emotions are tied to this role (resentment, guilt, obligation)? How does it affect how I see myself today?"

- **Prompt:** "What would it look like to step out of this role now? How might my relationships shift?"

2.Patterns of Behavior: Seeing the Invisible Cycles

Dysfunctional families often repeat patterns of conflict, avoidance, or control. These cycle scan leave lasting imprints.

- **Prompt:** "What recurring conflicts or behaviors in my family caused the most tension? How did they affect me?"

- **Prompt:** "How do I see these same patterns showing up in my life today (in my relationships, work, or self-talk)?"

- **Prompt:** "What one pattern do I want to break? What new, healthier pattern can I create to replace it?"

3.Relationship Dynamics: Mapping Closeness and Distance

Every family has a unique web of connections. Some feel warm and secure, while others feel distant or strained.

- **Prompt:** "Who in my family did I feel closest to, and why? What qualities made that relationship meaningful?"

- **Prompt:** "Who did I feel most distant from? What events, behaviors, or dynamics created that distance?"

- **Prompt:** "How might I heal or redefine these relationships? What boundaries or conversations would help?"

Interactive Exercise: Guided Visualization

Visualization can help you access memories and emotions that pure writing sometimes can't reach.

Guided Exercise:

Find a quiet space. Close your eyes and take three deep breaths. Imagine atypical family gathering from your past.

- **See:** Notice the setting. Where is everyone? What are their expressions and body language?

- **Hear:** What sounds are present? Laughter, arguing, silence, the clatter of dishes?

- **Feel:** What physical sensations arise? Tension in your neck? Warmth in your chest? A knot in your stomach?

Notice the emotions that surface without judgment. When you're ready, open your eyes and journal on these questions:

- "What dynamics or roles were most apparent in that scene?"

- "How did that experience shape my perception of family and connection?"

Emotional Safety and Compassion

Reflecting on these dynamics can be intense. Your well-being is the priority.

- **Create a Calming Space:** Light a candle, play soothing music, or journal in a place where you feel secure.

- **Pause and Ground:** If emotions feel overwhelming, pause. Place your feet flat on the floor, take five deep breaths, and name five things you can see.

- **Affirmation:** "I am reflecting to heal, not to dwell. This is a courageous step toward my growth."

Closing Reflection

As you close this chapter, take a moment to reflect. What patterns, emotions, or insights have emerged? Remember, healing is not a linear process; it's a series of small, intentional steps.

Your journal isn't just a collection of words; it's a map to your inner world. With each entry, you take another step toward understanding yourself and creating the life you deserve. You don't have to write perfectly; you only have to write honestly.

Affirmation:

"y journal is a safe space for self-discovery, reflection, and growth. With every word I write, I move closer to healing."

A Look Ahead:

The insights you've uncovered here are your foundation. In **Chapter 21**, we will build upon them with practical tools to turn your reflections into action. You will learn to build emotional resilience, set firm boundaries, and begin healing relationships, moving from understanding your past to actively creating your future.

CHAPTER 21
PRACTICAL TOOLS AND EXERCISES
Your Compass Through the Storm

Imagine standing at the edge of a stormy sea, waves crashing around you, each one representing a painful memory or unresolve demotion from your family. You feel overwhelmed, unsure of how to navigate the chaos. But what if you had a compass, a set of tools to guide you through the storm and into calmer waters? This chapter is your compass, offering practical strategies to help you heal, grow, and reclaim your power.

Navigating family dysfunction and emotional challenges often feels like trying to build a house without the right tools, frustrating, overwhelming, and seemingly impossible. But with the right techniques, you can dismantle old patterns, lay a strong foundation, and create a structure that reflects your values and aspirations.

These tools aren't just abstract concepts; they are practical steps you can implement in your daily life. Whether you're learning how to set boundaries, practicing mindfulness to calm emotional storms, or nurturing healthier relationships, each exercise is designed to help you reclaim your power and build the life you deserve.

Take a moment to reflect:

- *What areas of my life feel chaotic or unresolved?*

- *What would I gain by having the tools to address these challenges?*

This chapter will guide you in turning those questions into answers and those answers into action. You're not just reading about change, you're actively participating in it. Remember: the tools you practice today can transform the life you live tomorrow.

Call to Action

"As you move through this chapter, commit to trying at least one exercise that resonates with you. Each tool you pick up and practice brings you closer to the life you've dreamed of."

Building Emotional Resilience

Emotional resilience is your ability to adapt to stressful situations and recover from challenges with greater ease. It's not about avoiding difficult emotions but learning how to navigate them with grace and self-compassion. This section introduces practical tools to help you build emotional resilience and handle life's challenges with calm and clarity.

Tools and Techniques for Emotional Resilience
Grounding Exercises

- **5-4-3-2-1 Method**: This sensory grounding exercise is like planting your feet firmly in the earth during a storm.

- *How to Practice*: Identify five things you can see, four things you can touch, three things you can hear, two things you can smell, and one thing you can taste. This technique shifts your focus from overwhelming emotions to the present moment.

- *Example in Action*: Imagine being at a tense family gathering where emotions run high. Instead of spiraling, you silently name objects around the room: the flicker of a candle, the texture of your sweater, the murmur of conversation. Each observation pulls you back to the here and now.

Box Breathing

- *Description*: This is like pressing a reset button for your nervous system, calming the storm of emotions.

- *How to Practice*: Inhale deeply for four counts, hold your breath for four counts, exhale for four counts, and pause for another four counts. Repeat until you feel a sense of calm.

- *Practical Example*: Before a big presentation or family confrontation, practice box breathing to slow your heart rate and ground your emotions.

Personal Mantras

- *How to Use*: Identify a recurring negative thought and transform it into a positive affirmation.

- *Examples of Mantras*: *This is temporary. I am safe." "I can handle this moment with strength and calm."*

- *Interactive Exercise*: Reflect on a recent stressful situation and create your own mantra to reclaim your calm.

Progressive Muscle Relaxation

- *How to Practice*: Slowly tense and release different muscle groups, starting with your toes and working up to your shoulders. This helps release physical tension tied to emotional stress.

Visualization Techniques

- *Example*: Close your eyes and imagine yourself as a sturdy lighthouse in the middle of a storm. The waves crash around you, but you remain grounded, steady, and safe. This imagery reinforces your inner strength.

Cultural Sensitivity in Emotional Resilience

Emotional resilience might look different for everyone, shaped by cultural or generational norms. In some cultures, emotional regulation might involve silence and reflection, while others might embrace open expression. Reflect on how your upbringing has influenced your approach to emotions, and explore tools that align with your values.

Reflection Prompt

- *"What situations challenge my emotional resilience, and how can I prepare for them?"*

- *"What tools have I used before to regulate my emotions? Were they effective? How can I build on them?"*

Encouraging Self-Compassion

Emotional resilience isn't about being perfect; it's a skill that grows over time. It's okay to struggle at first. Each small step forward is progress. Remember: *"Every time you choose calm over chaos, you strengthen your ability to weather life's storms."*

Rewriting Your Narrative

Have you ever stopped to wonder how much of your life is shaped by a story you didn't write? Perhaps it's a narrative handed down by your family, shaped by the dysfunction you grew up with. These stories can whisper, *"You're not enough," "You'll never succeed,"* or *"You don't deserve love."* But what if today was the day you took the pen and began a new chapter, one written by your own hand, guided by your growth, resilience, and dreams?

The Emotional Impact of Limiting Beliefs

Limiting beliefs are more than just thoughts; they're emotional shackles. They can manifest as self-doubt, hesitation in relationships, or feeling 'stuck' in your personal or professional life. They often carry the weight of unspoken rules or expectations shaped by the dysfunction around us. These beliefs may have been survival tools in a chaotic environment, but as you grow, they become obstacles to living authentically.

Real-Life Example

"I was always told I wasn't smart enough," one woman shared, reflecting on her family's narrative. *"That belief followed me into adulthood, influencing every decision I made, until I decided it wasn't my truth anymore."*

Practical Tools for Rewriting Your Narrative

Rewriting your narrative isn't about ignoring the past; it's about reframing it. Here's how you can begin:

Identify Limiting Beliefs

Take a moment to write down the beliefs about yourself that feel restrictive or untrue.

Reflection Prompt: *"What story about myself have I been holding onto that no longer serves me?"*

Example: If you grew up being labeled as *"the quiet one,"* ask yourself, *"Is this true, or is this a label I've outgrown?"*

Reframe Your Story with Affirming Truths

For every limiting belief, write an empowering statement that aligns with the person you want to become.

Example: *"I'm not smart enough"* becomes *"I have the ability to learn and grow at any stage of life."*

Practice Self-Compassion

Treat yourself with the kindness you'd offer a friend.

Reflection Prompt: *"What would I say to my younger self to bring them comfort and encouragement?"*

Visualization Exercise: Close your eyes and imagine holding your younger self. Speak words of love and affirmation to them: *"You're safe. You're loved. You're enough."*

The Journey of Overcoming Resistance

Letting go of old narratives can feel daunting. Resistance may come from within, doubt, fear, or guilt, or from others who've benefited from your self-limiting beliefs. Here's how to navigate it:

- **Acknowledge Discomfort**: Growth often feels uncomfortable; it's a sign you're moving forward.

- **Start Small**: Reframe one belief at a time instead of overwhelming yourself with everything at once.

- **Seek Support**: Share your new narrative with a trusted friend, mentor, or therapist who can encourage and hold you accountable.

Deepening the Process with Visualization

Imagine stepping into a new chapter of your life. The air feels lighter, the colors around you seem brighter, and your shoulders relax as you shed the weight of old beliefs. What does this freedom feel like? What new possibilities do you see for yourself?

Visualization Prompt

"Picture a version of yourself who fully embraces your worth and potential. What are they doing? How do they carry themselves? What has changed?"

Gratitude as a Transformative Tool

Amidst the pain and challenges of rewriting your narrative, take time to reflect on the positive moments in your story. These moments, no matter how small, are the threads that weave resilience into your journey.

Reflection Prompt

"What strengths or joys have emerged from my experiences, even in difficult times?"

Reinforcement Strategies

Once you've rewritten your narrative, the work doesn't stop there. Consistency is key to making these new beliefs a natural part of your life:

- **Daily Reminders**

  - Write your new narrative and revisit it every morning. Use it as a grounding affirmation throughout your day.

  - *Example*: *"I am capable, resilient, and deserving of love."*

- **Affirming Actions**

  - Take actions that align with your new story. If you've reframed yourself as a capable leader, look for opportunities to lead, whether it's a project at work or organizing a community event.

Tying Narrative to Legacy

Rewriting your narrative isn't just about healing; it's about creating a foundation for the legacy you want to leave behind. Every belief you reframe, every choice you make, ripples out to inspire others.

Reflection Prompt

"What story do I want my children, friends, or loved ones to tell about me? How can I live that story today?"

Empowering Reminder

You are not bound by the stories you've inherited. You are the author of your life, capable of rewriting every chapter with courage, compassion, and vision.

Strengthening Boundaries

Boundaries are the foundation of healthy relationships and emotional well-being. They are the invisible lines that define your needs, values, and limits while honoring the individuality of others. For many coming from dysfunctional families, boundaries may feel foreign or even selfish, but they are a profound act of self-respect and protection.

The Power of Boundaries

Every holiday, Sarah found herself saying yes to tasks she didn't want to do, cooking, hosting, and even lending money. She often felt exhausted and resentful, but guilt kept her from speaking up. It wasn't until she learned the power of boundaries that she began reclaiming her peace. Today, Sarah confidently says, *"No, thank you,"* when a request doesn't align with her capacity, and she has rediscovered joy in spending the holidays with her family.

Emotional Benefits of Setting Boundaries

Setting boundaries is not about pushing people away; it's about creating space for respect, balance, and emotional well-being. Healthy boundaries protect your energy, reduce anxiety, and foster self-worth. They allow you to show unauthentically in relationships without feeling overextended or resentful.

Tools and Techniques for Strengthening Boundaries
Boundary Mapping: Identify Areas of Weakness

- Reflect on areas of your life where you feel drained, overwhelmed, or taken for granted. *Activity*: Divide a page into three columns: *Where I Feel Overwhelmed | Who or What Is Involved | What I Need to Change*

- *Example*: *"I feel overwhelmed at work when my boss assigns last-minute tasks. I need to communicate my limits and ask for more notice."*

Scripts for Setting Boundaries

- Having ready-to-use phrases can make boundary-setting less intimidating, especially in emotionally charged situations. *For guilt*: *"I appreciate that you need help, but I can't take this on right now. I hope you understand." For pushback*: *"I understand this might feel new, but this boundary is important for my well-being." For authority figures*: *"I want to do my best work and to do that, I need more clarity and time for this task." For loved ones*: *"I care about you deeply, but I need some time to recharge so I can show up fully."*

Reinforcement Strategies for Maintaining Boundaries

- Setting a boundary is just the first step; sticking to it is where growth happens. Calmly reaffirm your boundary if it's tested. *Example*: *"I know I've said no to this before, and that hasn't changed."* Reflect on why the boundary matters to you: *"This is about protect-*

183

ing my mental health, not rejecting the other person." Seek support: Share your boundary with a trusted friend or therapist who can hold you accountable.

Addressing Cultural and Familial Nuances

- Cultural and familial expectations can make setting boundaries challenging, especially in environments that prioritize collectivism or deference to elders.

- *Tip*: Start with small, respectful boundaries. For instance, say, *"I'd love to help, but I need to check my schedule first."*

- *Example*: Alex, raised in a culture that emphasized family loyalty, balanced tradition with personal growth by setting boundaries that honored both.

Quick Exercise: Start Small, Build Confidence

- *Reflective Prompt*: Write down one situation where you often feel overextended.

- *Action Step*: Identify a small boundary you can set in that situation this week.

- *Example*: If you feel overwhelmed by late-night texts from friends, decide to silence notifications after 9 PM and inform them of this change.

Boundary Myth vs. Truth

Myth: *"Setting boundaries is selfish."*

Truth: *"Boundaries are a way to protect both your energy and your relationships."*

Myth: *"Good relationships don't need boundaries."*

Truth: *"Healthy relationships thrive on mutual respect, which boundaries help establish."*

Affirmations with Visualization

- *Affirmation*: *"My boundaries protect my peace and honor my worth."*

- *Visualization*: Close your eyes and imagine setting a boundary with calm confidence. Picture the other person responding respectfully. Feel the sense of relief and empowerment that follows.

Reflection Prompt: Preparing for Challenges

- *What boundary am I ready to set, and how will it change my life?*

- *What challenges might arise, and how can I handle them with confidence?*

Overcoming Resistance with Empathy

- Remember, resistance is normal, especially if boundaries are new in your relationships. Approach these moments with empathy for yourself and others. *Example*: *"I understand this is an adjustment, but it's important for me to take care of my well-being."*

Empowering Thought

Setting boundaries is an act of self-love and respect. It's not easy, but with each step, you reclaim your peace and pave the way for healthier relationships. Remember, boundaries aren't walls, they're bridges to connection and understanding.

Healing Relationships

Relationships are the heart of our lives, yet they are often the source of our deepest wounds. Healing relationships doesn't mean ignoring past pain or pretending everything is fine. It's about navigating the path between understanding, forgiveness, and growth, whether that leads to repair or respectful distance. This section provides actionable tools to nurture meaningful relationships and explore the power of connection.

Practical Tools and Techniques for Healing Relationships
Active Listening Techniques:

- Healing begins with truly hearing others. Active listening fosters understanding and shows that you value the other person's thoughts and feelings.

- *How to Practice Active Listening*:

- Maintain eye contact and nod to show engagement.

- Repeat back what the other person says to ensure clarity: *"What I hear you saying is..."*

- Ask open-ended questions to encourage deeper conversation: *"How did that make you feel?"*

- *Example*: During a conversation with a sibling, instead of responding defensively to their criticism, pause and say, *"It sounds like you're frustrated about how things unfolded. Can you tell me more?"*

Conflict Resolution Skills

- Conflict is inevitable, but it doesn't have to destroy relationships. Constructive dialogue turns disagreements into opportunities for growth.

- *Steps to Resolve Conflicts*:

- Stay calm and pause to breathe before responding.

- Use *"I"* statements to express feelings without blaming: *"I felt hurt when..."*

- Seek common ground by asking, *"What solution feels fair to both of us?"*

- *Script for Navigating Conflict*: *"I know we've had some misunderstandings lately, but I value our relationship and want to work through this together. How can we approach this so we both feel heard?"*

Forgiveness and Rebuilding Trust

- Forgiveness is not about excusing harm; it's about releasing the hold that pain has on you. Rebuilding trust is a gradual process requiring effort on both sides.

- *Steps to Forgiveness*:

- Acknowledge your feelings without judgment.

- Separate the person from their actions; understanding their behavior reflects their struggles.

- Decide to forgive for your own peace, not theirs.

- *Steps to Rebuild Trust*:

- Identify and communicate boundaries for moving forward.

- Focus on consistent, small actions that demonstrate accountability.

- *Example*: A parent who frequently oversteps boundaries might earn trust by respecting your decisions over time without pushback.

Guided Visualization Exercise: Imagine a Healed Relationship

- Close your eyes and picture someone with whom you wish to heal. Imagine a calm, open conversation where both of you feel heard and respected.

- Visualize specific moments of understanding, like a sincere apology or shared laughter.

- Ask yourself:

- *What steps led to this connection?*

- *How did forgiveness and understanding play a role?*

- *What emotions arise as you imagine this healing?*

- Write down your reflections, noting small actions you can take to work toward this vision.

Relationship Check-Ins

- Regular check-ins foster ongoing connection and trust.

- *How to Check-In*:

- Schedule time to talk with loved ones about your relationship.

- Use open-ended questions, such as:

- *"What's one thing I've done recently that made you feel supported?"*

- *"How can we strengthen our connection?"*

- *Example Activity*: Share one thing you appreciate about each other during the conversation to build a foundation of positivity.

Handling Resistance or Unwillingness to Change

- Not every relationship will align with your growth journey. Recognize that healing doesn't always mean reconnection.

- *Steps to Navigate Resistance*:

- Accept that others may not be ready or willing to change.

- Focus on setting and maintaining your boundaries.

- Prioritize your own healing and emotional safety.

- *Affirmation for Support*: *"I release relationships that no longer serve me with gratitude and grace."*

Cultural Sensitivity in Healing Relationships

- Relationships are deeply influenced by cultural norms. Some families prioritize collective harmony over individual expression, while others emphasize independence.

- *Navigating Cultural Differences*:

- Acknowledge and respect your family's cultural framework.

- Balance traditional values with your personal growth by starting with small, respectful changes.

- *Example*: If direct confrontation feels inappropriate, use written communication to express your feelings or seek the support of a trusted family member to mediate.

Affirmations for Healing Relationships

- *"I have the courage to create relationships that reflect mutual respect and understanding."*

- *"I honor my boundaries and allow others to honor theirs."*

- *"Healing begins with small, intentional steps."*

Reflection Prompt

"What relationship deserves my effort and intentionality, and what is the first step I can take to heal it?"

Empowering Your Legacy

Building a legacy is more than an abstract concept; it's an intentional, ongoing practice of embedding your values into your daily life. This section ties the tools and exercises from this chapter to a greater purpose: creating a lasting legacy of love, growth, and connection.

Tools and Techniques for Legacy Building

- **Legacy Journaling to Articulate Values and Goals**

  - Journaling offers clarity on what truly matters to you. Write about the values you want to embody and the goals you hope to achieve.

  - *Prompt*: *"What one value would I want my loved ones to remember me for?"*

  - *Example*: Maria wrote about her goal to create a family culture rooted in kindness and respect. Over time, she turned her reflections into actionable steps, like practicing gratitude and active listening daily.

- **Family Rituals to Foster Connection**

Rituals bring people together and provide a sense of belonging. Whether it's a weekly gratitude circle, shared meals without distractions, or a monthly family check-in, these rituals strengthen bonds.

- *Reflection Prompt*: *"What ritual can I start today to bring more joy and connection to my family?"*

- *Example*: Jason initiated *"Thankful Thursdays,"* where his family shares one thing they appreciate about each other. It has become a cherished tradition.

- **Leading by Example to Inspire Change**

○ Actions speak louder than words. By modeling behaviors like patience, empathy, and resilience, you inspire others to follow suit.

○ *Real-Life Scenario*: Nina, a single mom, prioritized self-care despite her busy schedule. Her children observed her setting healthy boundaries and learned to advocate for their needs, too.

Reflection Prompt

"How do my daily actions reflect the legacy I want to leave?"
Write down three actions you've taken recently that align with your desired legacy. Reflect on how these small but meaningful choices contribute to lasting change.

Empowering Affirmation

"I am creating a legacy of courage, love, and authenticity. My actions today are planting seeds of growth for future generations."

From Tools to Transformation

Healing isn't a single destination; it's a continuous, transformative journey. Each tool and exercise in this chapter serves as a stepping stone toward building a life and legacy that reflects your deepest values.

Recap the Journey

You've explored tools for emotional resilience, rewritten limiting beliefs, set boundaries, and practiced healing relationships. Now, it's time to take action and integrate these practices into your daily life.

Reflection Prompt

"What tool am I most excited to try, and how will I incorporate it into my life this week?"

Take five minutes to reflect on the tools introduced in this chapter.

Choose one that resonates most deeply and plan one small step to put it into practice.

Creative Activity: Legacy Vision Board

For those seeking a creative way to engage, design a *"Legacy Vision Board."* Use images, quotes, and symbols to represent the values and actions you want your legacy to reflect. Display it somewhere visible as a daily source of inspiration.

Broader Impact of Legacy Creation

Your healing doesn't end with you. By choosing love and resilience, you ripple positive change into your community and future generations. One person's transformation has the power to inspire social healing on a larger scale.

Empowering Thought

"Healing is not a destination but a continuous journey, and every step forward is a step toward a brighter future. Every small action you take brings you closer to the legacy of love, courage, and connection you deserve."

Final Affirmation

"I am the author of my story, the architect of my legacy, and the embodiment of resilience and love. My journey is creating a brighter future for myself and those I touch."

CHAPTER 22

AFFIRMATIONS FOR EMOTIONAL STRENGTH

The Mirror of Self-Belief

Close your eyes and imagine standing before a foggy, cracked mirror. There flection staring back seems uncertain, weighed down by self-doubt and echoes of criticism. Now picture that mirror clearing and brightening until the person looking back at you stands tall, radiant with confidence. This is the power of affirmations.-

Affirmations are more than just words; they are tools of transformation. Like a gardener nurturing seeds into blossoms, repeating affirmations cultivates resilience, self-worth, and emotional strength. Neuroscience confirms that the brain rewires itself through repetition. Every time you affirm your worth, you carve new pathways of self-belief.

You may feel awkward at first. That's normal. Words once foreign or hollow eventually become your truth. This chapter will guide you in using affirmations to rebuild your inner voice, one empowering phrase at a time.

Start Here:

Write down one limiting belief you're ready to release (e.g., *"I'm not good enough"*). By the end of this chapter, you'll replace it with an affirmation that fuels your strength.

The Science Behind Affirmations

Why They Work

Affirmations are mental exercises that reshape your brain's neural wiring. Scientific research shows they:

- Lower stress hormones like cortisol

- Boost dopamine and motivation

- Interrupt and replace self-critical thoughts

- Strengthen emotional resilience over time

Real-Life Transformations

- **Maria**, who struggled with feelings of inadequacy, repeated *"I am enough exactly as I am."* Eventually, she stopped seeking external validation and began setting boundaries with confidence.

- **Jason**, who wrestled with anger, used *"I choose calm and kindness."* It gave him space to pause, reflect, and respond with empathy. His relationships transformed.

Myth vs. Truth

- *Myth:* "Affirmations are just wishful thinking."

- *Truth:* Affirmations are mental conditioning – like exercise for your mind. Repetition leads to transformation.

Crafting Personalized Affirmations
The Four Rules of Powerful Affirmations

1. **Present Tense** – "I am strong," not "I will be strong."

2. **Positive Language** – Say what you want, not what you're avoiding.

3. **Emotional Resonance** – Choose words that stir your spirit.

4. **Authenticity** – Start with affirmations that feel believable or aspirational.

Challenge Affirmation

Challenge	Affirmation
Self-Doubt	"I trust my wisdom and capabilities."
Anxiety	"I am safe in this moment."
Grief	"My love fuels my strength."
Burnout	"I honor my need for rest and joy."

Interactive Prompt:

Write one affirmation for each category that resonates with you. Keep them where you'll see them often.

Making Affirmations Stick

Daily Practices

- **Morning Power Start:** Repeat affirmations while brushing your teeth.

- **Mirror Work:** Look into your eyes and say them aloud.

- **Phone Reminders:** Set alerts with your affirmation at key times.

- **Evening Ritual:** Recite calming affirmations before bed.

Creative Reinforcement

- **Vision Board** – Add affirmations to inspirational images

- **Affirmation Jar** – Pull a slip of encouragement when needed

- **Mantra Music** – Turn affirmations into a short song or jingle

- **Touch Anchoring** – Pair your affirmation with a gesture (hand to heart, palm press)

Affirmations as Legacy

Affirmations aren't just personal healing tools; they're a legacy of strength.

Generational Healing

Teaching affirmations to children, friends, or partners helps build strong emotional foundations. Imagine your child repeating, *"I am loved. I am capable. I belong."*

Practical Ways to Share

- Recite affirmations together at dinner or bedtime

- Write affirmations on family notes or mirrors

- Establish a family ritual like "Gratitude + Growth" circle time

Legacy Prompt:

Write one affirmation you'd want to pass on to the next generation. (e.g., *"Int his family, we choose truth and tenderness."*)

Closing Empowerment

Affirmations are your anchor in storms and your compass in uncertainty. They don't erase hardship, but they change how you meet it. They're how you reclaim your narrative.

Final Challenge:

1. Choose one affirmation from this chapter

2. Repeat it 3x daily for one week

3. Journal how you feel at the end of the week

Final Affirmation:

"I am anchored in my strength, guided by my purpose, and resilient in the face of life's challenges."

Part Seven:

You're Ready Now

CHAPTER 23

SUMMARY OF LESSONS LEARNED

Imagine you've been climbing a mountain, step by step, through steep terrain and uncertain footing. At times, the summit felt impossibly far away. Yet, here you are, standing at a vantage point where you can see just how far you've come. You didn't just endure, you grew. Every challenge, every choice, and every moment of courage has led you to this point.

This chapter is your moment to pause and reflect. The lessons you've learned are more than insights; they are tools for transformation, guiding you into the next chapter of your life.

Take a moment to ask yourself: *What lesson resonated with you the most? How have these insights already started to shape your actions, your relationships, and your sense of self?* Healing is not a destination; it's an ongoing process, a series of small but meaningful choices that move you closer to the life you deserve.

As we explore the key takeaways from this book, you'll find these lessons woven into a toolkit you can carry with you. These tools are not just for navigating family dynamics but for every aspect of your life: setting boundaries at work, cultivating healthier relationships, and building a legacy of strength and compassion.

This is not just the conclusion of a book; it's the beginning of a new chapter in your life. Let's celebrate your progress, honor your resilience, and prepare to move forward with the clarity and confidence you've earned. Your story is far from over, and the best chapters are yet to come.

Key Lessons Organized by Theme

This section summarizes the key lessons from each part of the book, organized by theme. These lessons serve as a toolkit that you can use moving forward, providing actionable steps to create lasting change.

1. Understanding Family Dysfunction
- **Key Lesson**

Family dysfunction can feel invisible, like the air we breathe. We don't always recognize it because it's all we've ever known. But once we see it for what it is, we can begin to reclaim our power. The dysfunction we grew up with can sometimes feel invisible because it's been so ingrained in our lives. Family members may downplay or normalize behaviors that hurt, leaving you unsure of what's truly unhealthy. Recognizing these dysfunctional patterns, which are often passed down through generations, is the first step toward breaking free. Acknowledging dysfunction is an act of self-love, and the moment you see it for what it is, you reclaim your power.

- **Takeaway**

Begin by reflecting on the patterns in your own family. Identify behaviors that have been normalized but are actually harmful. Recognizing dysfunction is empowering. It means you no longer accept toxic dynamics as your truth. Start by understanding that change is possible, even if it feels overwhelming at first.

- **Reflection Prompt**

What is one family pattern you've identified as dysfunctional? How has recognizing this pattern empowered you to make changes?

2. Identifying the Problem

- **Key Lesson**: Dysfunction thrives in silence, miscommunication, and unspoken expectations. Recognizing the signs of dysfunction in your family dynamics, whether it's through passive aggression, lack of support, or an absence of healthy communication, is essential to healing. Identifying the problem is the first step to reclaiming your voice and your power. It's not just about recognizing dysfunction, it's about recognizing your role in breaking it. This process is empowering, even though it may initially feel like an overwhelming task.

- **Takeaway**: Practice active listening in your family conversations. Reflect on your role in communication, are you shutting down or engaging openly? Work on expressing your emotions and thoughts clearly, creating a space for healthier dialogue. Don't be afraid to call out dysfunctional behaviors, even if they've been a part of your family for years. Doing so will help shift the dynamic toward healthier, more honest communication.

- **Reflection Prompt**: *What is one communication pattern you'd like to change in your family? How can you take the first step toward healthier dialogue?*

3. Setting and Maintaining Boundaries

- **Key Lesson**: Boundaries are your safeguard against the emotional chaos of family dysfunction. Setting them is an act of reclaiming your peace, and maintaining them is a testament to your strength. Think of boundaries like a fence around your emotional garden. When you first put it up, it may be small and fragile. Over time, as you reinforce it, it becomes sturdier. But remember, family members might try to push against it, just like weeds trying to grow through your fence. Stand firm, your peace is worth it. Expect resistance, especially from family members who are used to crossing those boundaries. They may push back, test your limits, or try to guilt you into old patterns. But remember: boundaries are not just about keeping others in check; they are about protecting your peace. Stay firm, and with time, those who truly respect you will adjust. It may feel uncomfortable at first, but consistency is key in teaching others how to treat you.

- **Takeaway**: Start small by setting boundaries in less challenging situations. Gradually build your confidence in holding firm with more difficult conversations. Boundaries are not one-time declarations, they are a practice. Every time you reinforce them, you are strengthening your foundation for long-lasting change. Trust yourself, even when others try to test you. Your boundaries are a reflection of your self-worth, and you have the right to protect them.

- **Reflection Prompt**: *What is one boundary you've set recently? How did it feel to assert yourself, and what did you learn from the experience?*

4. Healing and Moving Forward

- **Key Lesson**: Healing is not about erasing your past; it's about transforming the way you relate to it. Healing may feel like two steps forward and one step back. You may find that old patterns creep back into your life, especially if family members continue to push old boundaries. But remember, setbacks don't erase progress. Healing is an ongoing process, and every effort you make, no matter how small, is a victory. Rebuilding self-esteem and redefining your relationships are acts of reclaiming your personal power. The key is in choosing growth over comfort and making consistent efforts to move forward, even when it feels difficult.

- **Takeaway**: Rebuild your self-esteem by practicing self-compassion. Use affirmations to remind yourself of your worth and give yourself permission to heal at your own pace. Embrace the idea that healing isn't linear, some days will feel like leaps forward and others like steps back. Each step you take is a victory, and you are constantly evolving. Focus on what you can control, and trust that your inner strength will guide you. Allow yourself to embrace the ongoing journey of healing and growth.

- **Reflection Prompt**: *What is one area of your life where you've seen growth? How can you celebrate that progress, even if it feels small?*

5. Practical Tools and Exercises

- **Key Lesson**: Tools like journaling, affirmations, and mindfulness exercises serve as powerful allies in the healing process. These tools help you process emotions, clarify thoughts, and create new neural pathways for healthier responses to family dynamics. They provide structure in times of emotional chaos and reinforce your resilience. The more you integrate these tools into your daily life, the stronger your emotional foundation becomes. Use these tools as a way to pause, reflect, and center yourself, especially when triggered by difficult family interactions.

- **Takeaway**: Use journaling as a way to explore your emotions, triggers, and experiences. For example, after a challenging conversation with a family member, write down the emotions you felt, the words that triggered you, and how you would have liked the conversation to go. Use this reflection to identify patterns and create a new script for how you'll handle similar situations next time. Commit to daily affirmations to foster a deeper connection with your inner self and build emotional strength. When faced with a difficult family interaction, try pausing, writing down your feelings, and giving yourself space to process before responding. These tools will help you reclaim your emotional power and build a more balanced and resilient mindset.

- **Reflection Prompt**: *What is one tool or exercise that has been most helpful to you? How can you incorporate it more consistently into your daily life?*

Quick Action List

After reflecting on each lesson, here are some quick action steps to take:

- **Understanding Family Dysfunction**: Reflect on one family pattern that you'd like to change. Write it down and consider how this pattern has impacted your life.

- **Identifying the Problem**: Practice active listening in your next family conversation. Notice any areas where communication breaks down, and reflect on how you can improve them.

- **Setting and Maintaining Boundaries**: Choose one small boundary you can set in your next family interaction. Practice asserting it calmly, and notice how it feels to stand firm.

- **Healing and Moving Forward**: Journal about one area of your life where you'd like to see growth. Reflect on what steps you can take, and give yourself permission to take those steps, even if they feel small.

- **Practical Tools and Exercises**: After any emotional or triggering family situation, take a moment to journal about it. Reflect on what went well, what didn't, and how you can approach it differently next time.

Emotional Connection

As you reflect on the lessons you've learned, it's important to honor the emotional journey you've been through. Healing from family dysfunction is no small feat. It requires courage, vulnerability, and a willingness to confront painful truths. You've already begun to change you family dynamics, and this healing journey isn't a one-time event; it's a process that continues with every choice you make. Every step you've taken has brought you closer to the life and relationships you've always deserved.

Hope and Empowerment

As we come to the final section of this book, take a moment to reflect on the incredible journey you've already embarked upon. What you've accomplished so far, acknowledging the dysfunction, setting boundaries, and healing old wounds, has been no small feat. Look at what you've already accomplished. You've faced challenges many would shy away from, and you've stepped forward with strength, courage, and determination. This is only the beginning of your powerful transformation. The healing you've experienced is real, and the work you've done so far has laid the foundation for even greater growth in the future.

Closing Reflection

As you close this chapter, remember: the work you've done is not just a step forward, it's a transformation. You have broken cycles, reclaimed your voice, and begun shaping a future aligned with your truth. This is only the beginning.

Be gentle with yourself. Celebrate your victories, no matter how small. Trust that your path is unfolding exactly as it should. Your journey is far from over, and I have no doubt that you will continue to rise, heal, and create the life you've always dreamed of.

CHAPTER 24

EMBRACING YOUR POWER TO CHANGE

A Moment of Transformation

What if I told you that the person you were yesterday no longer exists? That every step you've taken, every tear you've shed, and every moment of courage has brought you to this moment, a moment where you hold the power to create the life you've always dreamed of? Take a deep breath and feel the weight of that truth. This isn't just the end of a book; it's the beginning of a new chapter in your life. You are no longer defined by your past. You are here, now, standing at the threshold of endless possibilities.

Celebrating Your Progress

Take a moment to reflect on how far you've come. This journey has not just been about learning new lessons. It's been about the courage you've shown, the healing you've embraced, and the resilience you've built along the way.

You have faced hard truths. You have set boundaries that once felt impossible. You have chosen yourself, even when it was difficult. That is worth celebrating.

Growth is not always easy, and healing is never linear, but you have kept going. Now, as we reflect on the key lessons of this book, remember this: You are not the same person who started this journey. You are stronger, wiser, and more in control of your future than ever before.

Releasing Old Patterns and Beliefs

One of the most powerful aspects of embracing change is the ability to release old patterns and beliefs that no longer serve you. These patterns may have been deeply ingrained, passed down through generations, or formed as a result of past trauma. But just because something has been part of your life doesn't mean it has to remain there forever.

Releasing old patterns can feel like shedding an old skin, uncomfortable, raw, and vulnerable. But as you step into this new version of yourself, you will find freedom in the process. Let go of the beliefs that told you you're not worthy of love, not capable of success, or not deserving of happiness. These are just stories you've been told, and they are not your truth.

Action Step: Write down one old belief you're ready to release. Then, replace it with a new, empowering belief. For example:

- Old belief: *I'm not good enough.*

- New belief: *I am worthy of love, success, and happiness.*

Building a New Legacy

As you embrace your power to change, you're not just transforming your own life, you're building a new legacy. Think of this legacy as planting seeds in the ground. The work you do today, the boundaries you set, the healing you embrace, are like planting roots that will grow and flourish, leaving a foundation for others to build upon.

Your transformation sends ripples far beyond your immediate circle. As you heal and evolve, you contribute to a collective shift in your family, community, and even society. The healing you create doesn't stop with you; it begins to spread, encouraging others to embark on their own journey of transformation.

Action Step: Write down three actions you can take today to start building the legacy you want to create. For example:

1. Set a boundary with someone who drains your energy.

2. Practice self-compassion by speaking kindly to yourself.

3. Share your journey with someone who might benefit from your story.

Embodying the Change You Seek

Change is not just about thinking differently; it's about living differently. As you continue to heal and break free from old patterns, it's essential that your actions align with your new beliefs. You are no longer the person you once were, but in order to fully embody this transformation, you must begin to show up as the person you are becoming.

Start by looking at the small, everyday decisions you make. Every moment is an opportunity to practice the new version of yourself. Whether it's setting a boundary, practicing self-compassion, or taking time for self-care, these small choices add up. It's in these everyday actions that your transformation truly takes root.

Action Step: Visualize yourself waking up each day as the empowered person you are becoming. See yourself confidently setting boundaries, practicing self-care, and prioritizing your well-being. Write down one action you can take today to embody this vision.

Your New Beginning

Congratulations, you've made it. The work you've done, the challenges you've faced, and the transformation you've embraced have all led you to this moment. You've walked through fire and emerged stronger, wiser, and more aligned with who you truly are. Now, as you stand at the threshold of your new beginning, it's important to recognize that this is not an end, it's the start of something incredible.

Your journey has been one of profound change, but it's just the beginning. The past no longer defines you. The patterns of dysfunction, the fears, the doubts, and the limiting beliefs you've carried for so long are no longer your truth. As you step into this new chapter of your life, you are free to create a future that reflects your deepest desires, values, and goals.

Action Step: Close your eyes and imagine the life you want to create. What do you see? What are you doing? How do you feel? Write down your vision or create a vision board to keep it in your daily focus.

A Final Affirmation of Empowerment

As you take the next step in your journey, remember this: You are strong. You are capable. You are deserving of all the happiness and success you are creating. You have the power to change, and you will continue to transform into the best version of yourself.

Your Personal Affirmation: Take a moment to craft your own affirmation, one that speaks to your journey, your purpose, and your vision for the future. Write it down and let it be your reminder every day that you are worthy of the life you desire.

Closing Reflection and Next Steps

Before you close this book, take one action that symbolizes your commitment to change. Write down your biggest dream, say an affirmation out loud, or share your journey with someone you trust. This is your moment, claim it.

Reflect on these questions:

- What am I most proud of in my transformation so far?

- What obstacles did I face, and how did I overcome them?

- What action can I take today that will move me closer to my goals?

- How will I continue to prioritize my growth and healing in the weeks ahead?

Your future is shaped by the actions you take today. Reflect on your progress, and let that fuel the actions you take tomorrow. Every step you take is part of the new legacy you are creating. You are the creator of your own future, and now you have the tools to keep moving forward, one empowered choice at a time.

Final Personal Reflection: Your Story Is Just Beginning

"What's past is prologue." These words, written centuries ago, remind us that our history is not an anchor, it's a foundation. Every challenge, every lesson, every moment of courage has brought you here, to the threshold of a new beginning.

Think about how far you've come. The struggles you've faced, the pain you've healed, the lessons you've learned, they've all prepared you for this moment. But your story is not set in stone. You hold the pen now, and the next chapter is yours to create.

You are not bound by your past; you are informed by it. Every step you've taken, to understand, to heal, to grow, has brought you here. Now, you have the power to decide how your future unfolds. Every choice you make, big or small, shapes the life you are creating.

So, as you step forward, do so with intention. Embrace your power to create a life that reflects your values, your dreams, and your truth. Let go of fear, embrace possibility, and trust in the strength you've discovered within yourself. Take one small step today, write down a goal, set a boundary, or simply say "yes" to something that lights you up. This is your moment to begin.

Your past was the prologue. Your next chapter? That's entirely up to you. And as you turn the page, remember this: You are stronger, wiser, and more capable than you ever imagined. Your story is just beginning, and I have no doubt that it's going to be extraordinary.

Afterword
The Legacy You Choose

If you've reached this page, I want to honor you, not just for finishing this book, but for choosing yourself.

Healing from family dysfunction is not for the faint of heart. It requires courage to look backward, strength to feel what you were taught to numb, and audacity to believe in a future that looks nothing like your past.

I wrote this book because I've lived every chapter in it. I've known the ache of being silenced, the confusion of blurred boundaries, and the grief of realizing that the people who were supposed to protect me were the very ones who caused the most harm. But I've also known the power of healing, raw, imperfect, liberating healing. And I've seen firsthand what happens when a woman finally says, *"No more. It ends with me."*

You are not broken. You are not too much. You are not imagining it. The pain you carry has a history, but it does not have to define your future. Every insight you gained, every boundary you named, and every truth you reclaimed is part of a greater story, the story of your becoming.

This is not the end. It's a beginning.

You now have the tools. You have the language. You have the awareness. And with that comes power, the power to stop cycles, to raise your children differently, to love yourself unapologetically, and to build a legacy rooted in truth, not survival.

And because you've done this work, the legacy you leave will be different.

To Future Generations

May you inherit freedom instead of fear. May you know what safety feels like in your home, in your relationships, and within your own body. I did not walk through the fire so you would have to. I walked through it so you could be warm beside the flame, not burned by it.

May you grow up in a world where your voice is valued, your emotions are welcomed, and your boundaries are honored. If you ever wonder who changed things, know that someone before you said, *"Enough."*

I said enough.

For me.

For you.

For us all.

To My Daughter, Clarissa

My sweet girl, you are the reason I kept going. The reason I got up when life knocked me flat. I looked into your eyes and knew I had to become the woman I wished I'd had, so I could raise the woman I knew you'd become.

When you were twelve and told your friend, "I don't like how you're talking to me," I saw the cycle breaking in real time. You were proof that love could rewrite history.

If you ever feel uncertain, let this book remind you: you come from a line of women who were bent but never broken. And you, my love, are the promise that healing is possible. I am so proud of you, not just for who you are, but for who you are becoming.

A Final Word

As I often remind my clients: *"You may not have chosen the pain, but you get to choose the ending. And every time you choose healing, you rewrite the story for generations to come."*

Now, go write your ending.

With all my heart,

Juanita Kelly

Author, Trauma Recovery Specialist, and Fellow Survivor

About the Author

Juanita Kelly is a mental health educator, trauma recovery specialist, and founder of Bent Not Broken Books. With over 30 years of entrepreneurial experience and a Bachelor's and Master of Science in Psychology, she is currently pursuing her doctoral degree in Human and Organizational Psychology. Juanita blends academic training with real-life insight to empower women who have been silenced, dismissed, or broken by dysfunctional families, narcissistic abuse, and generational trauma.

She writes from the intersection of lived experience and clinical understanding. As a survivor of deep-rooted family dysfunction, Juanita knows what it feels like to shrink yourself for others' comfort, and what it takes to reclaim your voice, boundaries, and identity. Her writing is equal parts validating and practical, helping readers recognize toxic patterns, heal their self-worth, and build lives rooted in self-respect and emotional clarity.

Juanita is the creator of The Becoming Series, a bold and empowering collection of self-help books that guides women through the phases of emotional awakening, boundary-setting, healing, and reinvention after trauma. Her debut title, The Dysfunctional Family: How to Set Boundaries and Heal Yourself, serves as the foundation of the series and explores how to identify and break free from unhealthy family systems.

She is also the founder of Renew Behavioral Health, an upcoming trauma-informed mental health facility based in New Jersey, where her work will continue to center on the healing and empowerment of women and families. In addition to her clinical work, Juanita brings decades of leadership as a former fashion entrepreneur. For her work in fashion and business, she has previously been featured on MSNBC and on the covers of major regional publications, a creative legacy she now channels into helping women rewrite their stories and reclaim their light.

She currently resides in New Jersey with her husband and daughter, where she continues to write, teach, and lead healing spaces for women. Her mission is to transform her personal healing into a public revolution, offering not just awareness, but practical tools and the hope that no matter where you come from, you have the power to choose where you go next.

Recommended Resources

Books

The titles below were chosen to enrich and guide your healing journey. Each offers profound insight into emotional trauma, family dynamics, boundaries, and self-discovery. Whether you're seeking clarity, validation, or tools for lasting change, these research-backed works provide compassionate support.

- **Adult Children of Emotionally Immature Parents** by Lindsay C. Gibson
  Understand the lasting effects of emotionally immature parents and learn strategies to heal and reclaim your life.

- **Set Boundaries, Find Peace** by Nedra Glover Tawwab
  A straightforward guide to setting and maintaining healthy boundaries for greater peace and emotional well-being.

- **The Body Keeps the Score** by Bessel van der Kolk
  Explore how trauma affects the brain and body, and discover science-based paths to healing.

- **Will I Ever Be Good Enough?** by Dr. Karyl McBride
  A lifeline for daughters of narcissistic mothers, offering practical

tools to break free from damaging patterns.

- **Drama Free** by Nedra Glover Tawwab
  Learn how to manage toxic family relationships while safeguarding your mental health.

Online Resources

These trusted platforms provide mental health support, legal guidance, and identity-affirming care. Whether you're looking for a trauma-informed therapist or community-centered resources, help is available.

- **Psychology Today** – Search for trauma-informed therapists by location and specialty.

- **Therapy for Black Girls** – Find culturally competent therapists and healing resources.

- **Open Path Collective** – Affordable therapy for individuals, couples, and families.

- **NAMI** – Mental health education, peer support, and advocacy.

- **Love Is Respect** – Support for young people experiencing dating abuse.

- **Women's Law** – Legal help for survivors of domestic violence and abuse.

- **The Hotline** – 24/7 phone and chat support for domestic violence survivors.

Immediate Support Lines

- **988 Suicide & Crisis Lifeline**
  Call or text **988** for 24/7 free mental health and crisis support.

- **National Domestic Violence Hotline**
  Call **1-800-799-SAFE (7233)** or visit thehotline.org

- **Crisis Text Line**
  Text **HOME** to **741741** for free, 24/7 crisis counseling via text.

- **RAINN (Rape, Abuse & Incest National Network)**
  Call **1-800-656-HOPE (4673)** for confidential sexual violence support.

- **StrongHearts Native Helpline**
  Call **1-844-7NATIVE (762-8483)** for culturally grounded domestic violence support.

- **Trans Lifeline**
  Call **1-877-565-8860** for trans-led peer support.

Stay Connected

Juanita Kelly is committed to walking beside you as you reclaim your life. Visit her official website to stay connected and continue your healing journey.

Website: www.JuanitaKelly.com

Explore:

- Trauma Recovery Coaching

- Book Juanita for Speaking Engagements

- Media & Interview Requests

- Social Media & Podcast Updates

Coming Soon from The Becoming Series

The Dysfunctional Family Workbook

Designed as a practical companion to The Dysfunctional Family, this workbook features powerful journal prompts, boundary-setting exercises, and healing tools to help you break patterns, rebuild your identity, and start living life on your terms.

You're Not Crazy: How to Break Free from Abuse, Gaslighting, and Trauma Bonds

The second book in The Becoming Series helps you identify emotional manipulation in real time, understand trauma bonds, and reclaim your clarity. It's for the woman who's tired of feeling confused, dismissed, or emotionally stuck, and ready to name the abuse for what it is.

www.ingramcontent.com/pod-product-compliance
Lightning Source LLC
Chambersburg PA
CBHW031458120626
46545CB00005B/1665